GLOBAL VILLAGE AND
THE ECONOMY

GLOBAL VILLAGE AND THE ECONOMY

DR. YASH PAUL SONI

To order additional copies of this book, contact:
Xlibris
800-056-3182
www.Xlibrispublishing.co.uk
Orders@Xlibrispublishing.co.uk
731742

I wish to dedicate this book to my two grandchildren –
Arya (aged 14) and Ansh (aged 10).

Arya's passion is playing the violin and what pleasure
her performances have brought to our family. I feel
very proud she has already passed all her grade
exams with Distinction. As a member of the National
Children's Orchestra of Great Britain for the last three
years I have had the privilege to listen to her recitals at
the Royal Albert Hall and London's South Bank Centre.

Ansh is affectionately called 'Lil Tiger in the family due
to his passion to become a professional golfer. He is
on target to reduce his golf handicap to single digits
this year and has already won a significant number of
junior tournaments in both the UK and USA. His single
minded determination and practice ethic at such a

young age still never fails to impress me. He is focus and very motivated with his thought process, I am very sure one day he will rise to a very high position in his career.

Last but not least, I wish to express my deep gratitude to my Lovely wife Alka, for her patience and understanding during many months of strenuous work, even staying away for some time to complete this book. It gives me lot of comfort and pleasure now, that she is working and keeping herself busy with her own activities.

A very special thanks to everyone who has supported my work over the years, I am honoured by your trust and in awe of your vision for a better world. Through your presence, I have learned to become a better listener, and heard the words that allow me to share our empowering message of hope and possibility. To all, I remain grateful always.

PREFACE

The world today is home to a population of 7 and a half billion humans, and each human on our planet has his or her own unique way of interacting with one and other. Humans can interact privately, publicly or globally with each other. The efficient communication facilities that the humans are entitled to in today's date has definitely made the world a much smaller place.

Global human brain plays a massive role when it comes to the fundamentals of transformations of business economy. There are various sections of business economy and our population of seven and a half billion has unique ways of dealing with each.

The transformations that take place in cutting edge discernments when it comes to the nature of reality are considered as an archetype shift in the modern world of science. This book takes into consideration each side of my lifelong concerns and research and in a way, endorses every issue, opportunity, risk and challenge one may individually or collectively come across. It also slightly focuses towards the theoretical side of things, peeking into the boundaries of reality that resides in the development of the business world globally. Every conscious individual may need to invest his or her concerted efforts to solve the current global issues in this global village. Actions that have specifically been designed for maximum constructive impact must be chosen thoroughly. The entire global village has been going through several issues, and these issues can be related to either economy or simply any other issue from the variety of problems we have currently been facing. A few barricades exist that hinder one's ability to perform as per their motivation and vision.

The global economic stagnation when coupled with the unilateralism of the United States has debilitated or enfeebled the existence of the International Monetary Fund at the World Trade Organization. Regional economic agreements are now more significant and appealing compared to multi-lateral trade arrangements and trilateral trade with U.S.A. The frequency of trade increases and destabilizes as a result of this. The outcome of this can be noticed in the climate lately, wherein the new president of the United States has expressed his will to put a stop to supporting trans-pacific treaty. This decision would not go down well with the U.S. trade policy. The United States has also lately been making new agreements in NAFTA, and the reason behind this is once again the same. As soon as disruptions take place in the above mentioned agreements, the international economic system might get into fiascos. This global village actually requires two strong approaches, the first where every world leader would join forces immediately to help out the population, especially the most endangered ones, and secondly, to create a world-wide organization that would monitor the risks and consider the economic requirements of the people, as well as understand the rules of their local government. It would then be able to address a number of issues at the same time and hence, give rise to a global governance structure.

Many small and growing companies -- pioneers of business in the global village -- have discovered lucrative new markets abroad. Even developing countries are receptive to franchising, licensing and distribution. Not only are they enthusiastic importers of products and services, they are also eager to acquire the technological know-how and system support that comes from working with their international trading partners.

Although globalization has touched almost every person and locale in today's world, the trend has spread unevenly. It is most concentrated among propertied and professional classes, in the North (industrialized nations), in towns (urban areas), and among younger generations.

Globalization has not displaced deeper social structures in relation to production (capitalism), governance (the state and bureaucratic more generally), community (the notion and communitarianism more generally), and knowledge (rationalism). But, globalization has prompted important changes to certain attributes of capital, the state, the nation, and modern rationality.

In any discussion about globalization very few of the debate's participants deny the existence of the phenomenon. It is widely accepted that we all live in a globalizing world. The debates and protests emphasize how important it is to measure globalization. Without doing so, it is impossible to assess the severity or benefits of its effects and how it should be managed – if, in fact, it can even be managed. The winners and losers from structural changes that globalization seems to accelerate are the prime political actors in the debates.

TABLE OF CONTENTS

1. GLOBALIZATION

1.1. Introduction

The term "globalization" in the context of economics is a historical procedure, an outcome of the collaboration between current technological advancement and human creativity. It describes the ever-growing integration of economies, mainly via trade of goods, capital and other related services between countries all around the world. The term may also describe the transfer of knowledge (technology) and people (manpower) between countries. Globalization has several aspects, which include environmental, political and cultural dimensions.

It was the year 1980 when "globalization" became a widely-used term. Back then, it was used to refer to the technological advances which helped make international transaction processes easier, related to both, finance and trade. It also referred to the expansion of a market internationally, spreading to several other countries worldwide. These markets could include urban industries, rural markets or any sort of financial centers.

A number of signs show that in today's date, aspects such as people, goods and capital have globalized to a great extent, some of which have been mentioned below:

- In the year 1980, the trade value of goods and services as a percentage of world GDP used to be 42.1 percent, which jumped up to 62.1 by the year 2007.

- A great increase was noticed in foreign direct investment, which was 6.5 percent of world GDP in 1980 compared to 31.8 percent in 2006.

- A massive inflation took place in the stock of international claims (bank loans), which as a percentage of world GDP used to be 10 percent in 1980, touching 48 percent in 2006.

- In the year 1991, the total number of minutes spent on cross-border telephone calls used to be

7.3 per capita, growing up to 28.8 per capita in 2006.

- In the year 1965, the total number of foreign workers used to be 78 million (2.4 percent of the world population), which increased to 191 million (3 percent of the world population) in the year 2005.

This inflation in global markets has only given rise to greater competition and distribution of labor, indirectly improving efficiency. This type of specialization enabled economies as well as people to pay attention to and advance towards only those areas which they consider themselves experts in. Thanks to global markets, people can now be a part of markets that are bigger and more diversified all across the world. This leads to people gaining better access to the latest technology, more capital, reasonable imports and greater export markets. However, markets make no attempt to make sure that the advantages of better efficiency are shared by everyone. Every country must prepare to face any challenge and meet every requirement they may have to. If a country is not too strong financially, it should look for ways to collaborate internationally, seeking help from the international community while ensuring that the preparations are not hindered.

The great wingspan of globalization even reaches as far as everyday choices regarding economic, personal and political life. For instance, if modern technologies in the context of health care became more accessible, more lives could be saved. In the context of communications, education and commerce could greatly benefit and an independent media might develop. Globalization could also mean better co-operation between countries regarding a variety of non-economic issues which may have cross-border inferences, for example immigration, environment and other legal complications. Besides, inflow of foreign services, items and capital into a country could lead to better education systems as the citizens of the country might start realizing the level of competition they may have to face, giving rise to more incentives and greater demands.

Essentially, globalization also tries to suggest that knowledge and information should and do get distributed and shared. For example, innovators could make use of an idea that was once successfully implemented and revamp the same idea however they wish to, basically taking a leaf out of someone else's book. Even better, they could either ignore or completely revamp ideas that have completely failed in the past. However, a Nobel laureate named Joseph Stiglitz, who is also a known globalization critic has claimed that globalization "has lowered the overall sense of isolation noticed in a majority of the developing world, and has granted a number of people from developing nations access to the kind of knowledge not even the wealthiest from any countries might be aware of a hundred years ago".

1.2. Aspects of Globalization

Here are the different aspects of Globalization. This will help us understand how Globalization affects our day to day lives.

1.2.1. Industrial Globalization

Specialization, a term that is used to describe the process of manufacturing only those products that have shown signs of competitive advantage when it comes to cost in a particular country, is something all the countries are currently striving towards. For instance, the United States is known to specialize in military equipment, while Singapore is known for pharmaceutical products. Hence, all the countries trade their industrial products and thereby meet the demands of their populace. There is a heavy interdependence between countries, and each country relies on other countries for trade and resources. Currently, the US holds the title for the biggest economy worldwide, but it still depends on several countries to fulfill a variety of its needs. Therefore, the industries that presently operate do not just help fulfilling their home country's needs, but they help fulfill needs of other countries all around the world as well. This is what we know as Industrial Globalization.

Besides, in order to ensure quality, numerous standards have been established which every country involved in trade and exchange must meet. The ISO 9000 standards are the most widely known and followed quality standards all around the world. Things have changed, and today, markets worldwide have all collaborated, due to which products can now be traded and sold anywhere with no obstructions. To sum it all up, Industrial Globalization can be defined as the rapid growth of production markets all around the world and a greater access to a variety of products for companies and consumers.

1.2.2. Financial Globalization

This category of Globalization can be defined as the growth of financial markets all around the world and domestic, national and corporate debtors gaining greater access to external financing. For instance, foreign investors fully sponsored projects such as Mangle Dam and Tarbela Dam that had taken place in Pakistan. These foreign investors could either be independent individual investors or international organizations. Moreover, the World Bank and the IMF today grants much needed financial aid to countries in order to help them carry out developmental projects.

Hence, in simpler terms, Financial Globalization refers to the fact that financial markets all around the world have now joined forces, as a result of which financial help is available to any country in need with no hassle.

1.2.3. Political Globalization

This category of Globalization has a simple meaning. It can be defined as the rapid development of political interests of one country in several other countries. For example, the discussion regarding America's next President takes place not just in America, but in all parts of the world. American president has lot of plans and the whole world is concerned, how he is going to put them in action, for examples two of his plans are now in competition. The first is the relatively general platform that Trump issued during the campaign and hasn't updated. The second is the more comprehensive House Republican proposal. The two are remarkably similar, with one huge exception; The house plan includes a complex, controversial measure called the BAT (border adjustment tax) which has the potential to raise a massive $1 trillion in tax revenue.

1.2.4. Informational Globalization

This globalization aspect probably affects and benefits the world more than any other aspect. For example, you could be living in Australia, and could gain access to information available in America, and you would not even have to make any efforts to do so. We now have the internet, telephone, television and so much more, all of which allow us to get information in a matter of seconds right from our homes. The flow of information has improved so radically around every part of the world that we no longer are unaware of what has been happening in various parts of the world, be it a geographically remote region. In short, the simple and fast availability of information regardless of location is known as Informational Globalization.

1.2.5. Cultural Globalization

This category of Globalization, which is to be looked at in the context of Organizational Psychology, refers to the rapid growth of cross-cultural communications. Our world was and is home to numerous cultures depending on the location. The only difference is that, these cultures never got along in the past but are now taking inspiration and influence from one another, starting to become similar and friendlier with each other. The overall environment mankind is currently living in has transformed and improved, and cultural barriers no longer affect us. This is what we know as Cultural Globalization.

1.3. Trends associated with Globalization

1.3.1. The Liberalization of Governmental Trade Policies

Globalization may not be entirely logical, but it is also inevitable at the same time. A nation or a business cannot just isolate itself, neither can it possess a commerce that is fully unregulated. Regulation is required, but the only question is how much of it do we need, and what type of it are we looking for. The government comes up with standards for international trade and regulates the overall structure of international trade, figuring out which particular sectors need to be privatized. This way, the government plays a huge part in globalization. Moreover, International Monetary Fund loan terms demand particular sectors to go private.

A country is said to be globalized if the government actively expedites investment. Resources should be allocated freely in a marketplace, and the atmosphere should be accordingly suitable. Hence, the primary objective of the government must be to come up with an efficient marketplace by granting a better framework of corporate governance and business laws, establish an economic framework that is more stable, and grant better supply-side flexibility at micro levels (Alexander and Warwick, 2007). It was stated by Kagan in 2007 that globalization has definitely dominated the autonomy of national governments, forcing legal systems of economically advanced democracies in the way of convergence. Convergence has to exist between governments because only then can trade be effectively regulated in all the countries involved. Lately, laws regarding trade are turning more liberal in a number of ways, allowing new countries and regions to actively take part in trades. This is what we need in order to allow more regions to get involved in trading, which eventually improves the economic growth. Lately, the United States was noticed to maximize its membership in intergovernmental organizations and has also maximized the overall legislations passed which were originally made to regulate various aspects of finance and trading (Pryor, 2000). Thanks to this new standardization, the United States can now trade freely and more regularly with other nations. The newcomers in the world of trading can now make products that are more affordable for the citizens of the United States. It is quite significant for developing nations to actively take part in trade agreements so they too could gain some sort of competitive advantage in a world that has reached such an extent of globalization. It has been suggested by a research that liberalization needs to progress further in both, developing as well as developed countries so that every country could make the best out of globalization.

Moreover, financial capital is now of major significance as well, making it quite important for organizations to increase shareholder value in order to positively impact the functioning and distribution of wealth and income within the company. As a result of deletion of the Bretton Woods agreement, financial deregulation has taken place and exchange markets have turned hypothetical and now depend on the total money that flows throughout the system instead of overall trade flows (Went, 2004). As capital now flows freely throughout the financial markets of the world, technology as well as trade have undergone a massive outburst. For instance, an investor could loan some money from a bank located in London and could use the funds to construct a huge building in China, and could at the same time have financial help from investors in Dubai, Sweden, and Australia. As I have mentioned in my earlier notes about the BAT, it is the Revolutionary new border tax that resembles the VAT, or value-added tax, levied by virtually all of American trading partners. The BAT, however, is a different animal.

1.3.2. Increase in Inequalities among Nations

Inequalities among nations have notably increased as a result of globalization. Literature has a number of gainsaying perspectives regarding the current state of inequality being faced by nations and how these inequalities get affected by globalization. The wealthiest nations keep on improving their capitals but at the same time, the less fortunate nations continue to get poorer. It was noted that about 20% of the wealthiest population of the world handle 86% of world GDP and 82% of world exports, while on the other hand, 20% of the poorest population consume 1.3% (Herriott and Scott-Jackson, 2002). It was predicted by (Crafts, 2003) that a steady increase will be noticed in the growth rates for new countries that have only started taking part in international commerce. According to him, countries that are not wealthy will not miss out on globalization as trade borders keep reducing all over the world, including fiscal stability and creation of macroeconomics, and also ease trade managements substantially (Graham, 2001). With the help of these reforms, nations can collaborate more effectively into the global world and thereby lower the inequality that currently exists between the U.S. and the rest of the nations that are already a part of the global marketplace. Developing and emerging countries such as China and India have reduced overall poverty and have improved their economic growth significantly ever since they implemented economic policies in the 1990s (Cheng and Mittlehammer, 2008). This goes to show that developing nations can also make the best out of globalization and avoid side effects if they adopt the right policies. Hence, it becomes important to make use of these policies effectively so more and more countries manage to get the benefit of globalization. If developing countries are assured that they may not have to face any sort of inequalities if they joined globalization, they would want to try it out. The United

Nations Conference on Trade and Development (UNCTAD) in 1995 carried out an empirical research in developing countries situated in Asia. The outcome of this study showed them that foreign investments played a major role in improving economic growth if country-specific aspects such as school attainment, domestic financial development and national income are taken into consideration (Carkovic and Levine, 2002). Numbers show that joining globalization is completely harmless for developing nations, but a number of researchers still suggest that it may not be entirely harmless. This study may be a bit lop-sided given the factors we have considered. Researches might have mixed data up when they used the information from the past conditions of a country, comparing them to current conditions. A few of these countries could have been so bad off right since the start that it looks like there is in fact a positive impact on the economy of that country.

Every country that wishes to follow the path of globalization must come up with local conditions to support their decision. These conditions may include, establishing a well-functioning and stable financial market, developing quality institutions, and creating human capital. These institutions must thoroughly be utilized by the government in order to develop better policies and offer public services more effectively. But according to literature, the quality of institutions impacts quantity as well as quality of input productivity. It was noticed in a research that the institution quality impacts investment rate of capital as well as stocks (Gwartney et al., 2004).

According to some researchers, even though globalization has the ability to help improve every nation involved, it fails. According to Basu (2003), "those who currently find themselves at the pinnacle of global economics and politics have ensured that their capital gets accumulated and grows, also protecting their power secretly". That said, those countries which are still new to globalization fall victim to inequality and suffer.

1.4. Negatives of Globalization

The greatest disadvantage of globalization is that it continues to increase the difference between the poor and the rich. It is clear that the rich continue to become richer while the poor become poorer. Due to outsourcing, globalization might kill job opportunities as well as resources of an entire nation. This happens due to the fact that globalization has to take jobs away from one country and grant it to another, stealing opportunities from many. Even though people from different cultural backgrounds and nations get to interact with one and other, tradition and values face a big loss. Species do not get to stay with their native ecosystems and the chances of diseases spreading increase, leading to disruptions in other ecosystems and the species native to them.

1.5. Regional economic integration

Regionalization is yet another widely-known aspect in today's date apart from globalization. The word "region" could have several meanings to it. In this context, it is used to refer to an entity encircling and outdoing nation-states, and most likely including hegemony, which is also a type of nation-state.

1.5.1. Progress of Regionalization

Even though the imperialist authority wished to include and unite multiple regions of the world which had always stayed away from each other independently, it was modern capitalism that led to the forging of deeper relations between those regions, eventually leading to the unification of the entire world. The regions all stayed the same and did not disappear, and have surely continued to represent and emphasize their original identity. Regionalization is a term that refers to this persistence of identity. Regionalism is the principle of promoting this advance.

The growth and popularity of the term regionalization has started to rack up a lot of attention, mainly ever since the U.S. hegemony started to diminish. Even though it varied in terms of importance, character and scale from one region to another, regionalization kept on progressing on a global scale after the late 1980s and kept going until the early 1990s. Regionalization's economic aspects could be defined as the attempts to create free-trade zones, and with the establishment of common markets, implementation of joint economic policies and collaboration of these economic policies, even bigger economic zones could be established. This trend is mainly encouraged by the European Union (EU) and European Community (EC) in Western Europe,

North American Free Trade Agreement (NAFTA) in North America, Mercado Comun del Cono Sur (MERCOSUR) in South America, and the Association of Southeast Asian Nations (ASEAN) in Asia. They continue to encourage this trend, and attempts have also been made to unify at the Pan-Pacific level to create the Asian Pacific Economic Cooperation Conference (APEC).

Similar to globalization, regionalization also has a great effect on the nature of nation-states. Regionalization has left a huge impact on the predominant hegemony as a type of nation-state by extension. Regionalization has also left a regulating impact on several multinational organizations via standards such as corporate laws, labor policies and competition policies. In some instances, this impact has turned into a form of retaliation against multinational companies by combined nations. On the other hand, relations among regional organizations, such as interregional relations, have turned more significant as a façade of international relations as a whole.

1.6. Employment Disparity

Globalization has introduced greater equality to the world. Transport continues to get faster, communication continues to get cheaper, and developing countries are slowly getting on the level of developed ones. But inside of various developing economies, the stories aren't as pleasant. Inequalities have actually grown. A measure of inequality known as the Gini index, which is based on a score between 0 and 1, states that the entire income of a country goes to just one person if the score is 1, while it states that the income is equally divided if the score is 0. Sub-Saharan Africa noticed a 9% inflation in its Gini index between 1993 and 2008. The Gini index of China inflated by 34% in a time frame of twenty years. It has fallen only in certain regions. So what does globalization have to do with this?

Economists believe globalization plays no part in this. According to basic theory, inequality reduces when developing countries choose to enter global markets. Every introductory textbook includes the theory of comparative advantage. It mentions that countries that are poor produce goods but demand a high number of unskilled labor, while on the other hand, rich countries look for skilled workers instead. For instance, America is the biggest exporter of financial services in the world, while Thailand is the biggest exporter of rice. While global trade continues to increase, as per what the theory mentions, unskilled workers from poor countries are in great demand; while skilled workers in those countries aren't looked for. Unskilled workers continue to get bonuses in developing countries, while skilled workers don't. As a consequence, inequality reduces.

New theories continue to show up as a result of high inequality seen in poor countries. One of these theories talks about outsourcing; when rich countries transfer their production processes to poor countries. Contradictory to the mainstream belief, multinationals located in poor countries tend to look for skilled workers and pay them well. According to a study, workers in foreign-owned footwear and clothing factories in Vietnam are a part of the top 20% of the country's population by household expenditure. According to a report from OECD, the average wages that foreign multinationals pay are 40% greater than what the local firms pay their workers. Moreover, these skilled workers get a chance to work along with managers from other rich countries and might have to meet the deadlines of a company belonging to a rich background and country. That boosts the productivity as well. Greater productivity leads to workers demanding greater wages. On the other hand, poor workers from rural regions and other unskilled workers do not get any of these opportunities and can expect nothing in return to a rise in productivity, if that is even possible for them. Therefore, globalization can surely make the skilled workers richer, but at the same time making poor workers poorer. Inequality hence increases.

There exist several other economic theories that try to discuss about how inequality has reached new heights in developing countries. Simon Kuznets, a Nobel laureate has stated that the increase of inequality was completely unavoidable during the early stages of development. According to him, anyone who possessed enough money to invest could expect great returns and would hence get richer as growth progresses, but those who had nothing would remain poor and may only get poorer. Inequality would fall only if the economy was developed and a demand for redistribution arose. As per the recent evidence, inequality may not be rising now as quick as it once rose in developing countries, which gives rise to new questions for the economists. But given the current circumstances, it is going to be a challenging task to fight inequality in developing countries that emerges as a consequence of globalization.

1.7. Pro-Globalization

This term refers to standards that embolden open communication, trade and allow people to move to different countries with no restrictions. Companies, individuals and organizations are said to be a part of pro-globalization if they encourage policies like open borders, off-shored production, etc. and do not approve of restrictions such as impediments, tariffs and other such political and economic restrictions imposed by governments.

1.8. Signs of Globalization

Critics of free market economics such as Ha-Joon Chang and Joseph Stiglitz have always been targeting globalization, trying to prove that globalization propagates inequality. Some have started to believe that these critics may be right, after all. According to a report by the International Monetary Fund in 2007, it was noticed that inequality levels have actually grown as a result of new technology being introduced and foreign capital being invested in developing nations. Moreover, there are people in developed nations who do not approve of globalization either. They believe that globalization enables employers to transfer jobs away to developing places, which they find cheaper. "Delocalization" and "Globalization" are already considered derogatory terms in France in context of free market policies. According to a pollster that was a part of an April 2012 survey carried out by IFOP, 78% of the French people felt that globalization was "bad" for their country.

Besides, economic historians have been trying to question whether the advantages of globalization overshadow the drawbacks, a question we find very difficult to answer. They believe that the answer depends on when according to you did globalization first begin. But then again, does it matter if globalization actually started two or even two thousand years ago? They respond to this by saying that one cannot measure how successful a process has been without defining the amount of time it has been running for.

Economics from the past probably were well aware of the fact that people and markets all across the globe were integrating more as years went by. Even though Adam Smith never really used the exact term, globalization is a pretty significant theme in the Wealth of Nations. He uses the example of integration of markets over time as the underlying principle for his description of economic development. Labor gets divided, leading to an increase in the output, which further leads to a hunger for specialization. This promotes trade and eventually integrates communities from the remote regions of the globe. This is a type of trend which may be as old as civilization. Primitively, labor still used to get divided between "shepherds" and "hunters", and this division kept growing as trading networks and villages continued to expand in order to enable greater specialization. In time, division of labor became a very common occurrence, for instance armorers to craft bows and arrows, seamstress to make clothing items, carpenters to construct houses, etc. came to be known as specialist artisans, and started trading their creations for food that the hunters and shepherds managed to gather. Markets grew more and more integrated as continents, countries, towns and villages started to trade goods they could efficiently produce for goods they cannot or did not know how to produce, encouraging trade and specialization. Even though back then the geographical area covered as a part of "globalization" as described by Smith was nowhere as widespread as the area being covered presently, one would still call it globalization.

1.9. Cultural Deterioration

After considering what has been discussion above, one could say that the analysis of how globalization has impacted culture does not help understand the concept of globalization in terms of an increase in the exchange flows of worldwide trade, neither in the sphere of financial and capital flows nor in the sphere of merchandise. Even though one could agree that in the maximization in trade, there exist certain goods that could be considered rather cultural, for instance, musical works, books, furniture designs and themes, etc. and we have already discussed how the culture an object belongs to or has originated from can never be ignored.

The current instance that different nations have different access to new technologies and the rapid increase in distance between the excluded and the included is not a cultural instance. It could be a possibility that an updated awareness regarding the overall value of information and an increase of trade activities in imperceptible items further proves that the ability to increase the value of the goods appropriately is what creates a difference in the levels of productivity among nations, between certain regions of the globe and among production facilities inside a country. But this is nothing new because the inception of the new world, wherein interest on money was taken as a proper gain and not moneylending, led to the opening of a whole new path towards social differentiation originating from a monetary economy with its resulting compulsions of competitiveness and efficiency to achieve the highest possible value of goods. It could probably be said that this differentiation has gone up to such an extent that it is just not reversible anymore, because of which ideologies that claimed that human equality was the reason behind all the efforts that the political community made are not relevant anymore. But due to the reasons discussed above, the concept of equality is simply an observation approach that does have a blind point, and may not be able to get rid of the inconsistency that the observer is not being able to notice on either side of the differentiated. The question that asks about how equal the equals really are boggles people's minds every day in the most diverse contexts, mainly due to the fact that they experience this behind equality approaches, and differentiations are traced by the society itself.

1.10. Rise in Health Risks

While one may be aware about the economic benefits of globalization for countries, they might be completely ignoring the health challenges that the people of those countries could have to face. This is the message a new report by the World Health Organization tries to convey, a report that was published to overlap with the World Health Day, a day that is celebrated every year on the 7th of April. The day marks the anniversary of WHO's founding, which took place in the year 1948.

Iain Simpson, the spokesman for WHO stated in a conference that had taken place in Singapore regarding World Health Day that there exists an increasing amount of health issues related to the increasing number of goods and people crossing borders every single day, because these goods and people may carry diseases along with them. He went on to say that countries must introduce additional international health security for enhanced protection.

WHO released yet another international health security report, wherein it has pointed out the following priorities for itself:

Influenza and SARS, some of the most threatening infectious diseases that are currently spreading; diseases that have recently been spreading all around the world more easily as a result of people and goods moving to different countries as a part of global economy; management of international health disasters, similar to earthquakes and tsunamis; AIDS; the impacts of global warming; awareness of biological and chemical terror threats.

Simpson stated that this list is not entirely prioritized but is simply a compilation of problems, all of which are equally worthy of attention. These issues are a major part of the threat that international health security currently faces.

According to Simpson, during the last decade, the risk of diseases spreading has grown as global trade increased. Even though commercial goods are transferred and people consider it to be a good thing, they fail to notice that these commercial goods may include contaminated food items, black market goods that are illegal, diseases, etc.

However, the growing possibility of an international flu pandemic and the SARS epidemic that had already taken place in 2003 are two of the most feared events as of now, according to Simpson.

SARS (Severe Acute Respiratory Syndrome) kicked off in the fall of the year 2002 in China, and managed to kill about 800 people all around the world, mainly in Asia before it faded away in the consequent Summer. Even though the world managed to stop the disease from spreading further, Simpson said that the pandemic acted as a wake-up call regarding the possibilities of more such threats showing up in the near future.

These global issues are nowhere close to the international issues back in the days that encouraged the founders of the United Nations to establish the WHO after the World War II concluded, as per Simpson's words.

Simpson stated that when WHO was first established similar to the rest of the United Nations agencies, people worried more about obtaining world peace, and eliminating health issues was a part of this ideology. A person being in Malaysia at 9 AM in the morning and being in London the very next day was not a possibility when the WHO was formed in 1948.

1.11. Globalization in question

When speaking of globalization, one question that comes to mind would be if there is a possibility to reverse globalization, and if yes, how reversible is it. In this case, reversing does not refer to whether globalization can be altered to the extent of complete demobilization. Instead, it refers to whether globalization can be altered in such a way that all societies find it possible to make the best out of it, and not just a few countries. In order to analyze this question, one would have to take a proper look into the unfair nature of today's globalization and the way it treats nations, and then come up with ideas to adjust it so nobody has to face any side effects. The World Commission on the Social Dimension of Globalization has urged nations to be entirely conscious and mindful about the possible risks of encouraging globalization, while advancements are very distant for many (The Association for Women's Rights in Development, 2008).

Capital is being amassed, but there also exist development related issues such as poverty, inequality and exclusion. Normally, bribery is a common occurrence, violence endangers free and open communities and cultures, and the question whether open markets should exist remains unanswered. Global sovereignty is in a dilemma as of now. We are at an unsafe stage of decision making, and we really need to revamp our current policies and organizations taking every possible aspect into consideration (The Association for Women's Rights in Development, 2008).

Societal change has always been a thing, and societies have changed enough for mankind to be able to achieve a lot. Had it not been for social changes such as medical discoveries, technological advancements, etc. it would barely be possible for mankind to even survive. But then again, societal change is not always beneficial. Similarly, globalization may have its benefits and advantages, but we cannot ignore the disadvantages that come along with it. Countries like the United States enjoy its fortunes while Africa continues to struggle. The concept of globalization is hence rather unpredictable. Currently, Africa greatly depends on farming and exports for its economy, which will become a rather outdated practice as a result of globalization.

Financial experts believe that globalization and advancement towards an informational market which depends upon knowledge-based items might worsen Africa's already precarious position in the global market (IPS 2004). As of now, the economy of Africa depends greatly on regionally grown commodities like cocoa, sugar, vanilla, palm oil, etc. and is all about coming up with better techniques to produce faster and cheaper, while also staying within "research facilities or within the non-traditional environment" at the same time (IPS 2004). While a majority of the world looks forward to globalization and gets excited about it, African farmers and some others fear economic destructions and dark days. Globalization has already started to destruct the nature of equitable commerce.

Hence, the current process needs various alterations to make sure none of the countries suffer as a result of globalization. The Commission came up with a multifaceted task in its document which named "A Fair Globalization", and does the job of creating opportunities for whoever matches the following criteria:

- More attention towards people who address global issues such as community empowerment, gender equality, work opportunities, cultural autonomy, etc.
- A state that is both effective and democratic wherein there exists a capacity to offer social and economic opportunities to everyone while assimilating into the global economy.
- Maintainable growth in environmental, economic and social aspects.
- Fair set of rules and regulations.
- Markets that are equitable and productive.

- Globalization inspired by solidarity.
- A United Nations that is rather effective and appropriately enforces a system of governance that makes a difference.
- Greater partnerships in every organizational level.
- Higher responsibility towards citizens, both private as well as public.

To sum it all up, these proposals suggest a democratic approach and a greater participation of nations and its people in the creation of policies that they will be depending on in the future. They also wish for those who possess enough authority such as businesses, laborers, governments, parliaments, civil societies, and international organizations to get to know their responsibilities and do everything in their power to encourage an equitable, free and productive global community (The World Commission on the Social Dimension of Globalization, 2004).

2. THE GREAT DIVIDE IN THE GLOBAL VILLAGE

2.1. Incomes are Diverging

MAINSTREAM economic thought promises that globalization will lead to a widespread improvement in average incomes. Firms will reap increased economies of scale in a larger market, and incomes will converge as poor countries grow more rapidly than rich ones. In this "win-win" perspective, the importance of nation-states fades as the "global village" grows and market integration and prosperity take hold.

But the evidence paints a different picture. Average incomes have indeed been growing, but so has the income gap between rich and poor countries. Both trends have been evident for more than 200 years, but improved global communications have led to an increased awareness among the poor of income inequalities and heightened the pressure to emigrate to richer countries. In response, the industrialized nations have erected higher barriers against immigration, making the world economy seem more like a gated community than a global village. And although international markets for goods and capital have opened up since World War II and multilateral organizations now articulate rules and monitor the world economy, economic inequality among countries continues to increase. Some two billion people earn less than $2 per day.

At first glance, there are two causes of this divergence between economic theory and reality. First, the rich countries insist on barriers to immigration and agricultural imports. Second, most poor nations have been unable to attract much foreign capital due to their own government failings. These two issues are fundamentally linked: by forcing poor people to remain in badly governed states, immigration barriers deny those most in need the opportunity to "move up" by "moving out." In turn, that immobility eliminates a potential source of pressure on ineffective governments, thus facilitating their survival.

Since the rich countries are unlikely to lower their agricultural and immigration barriers significantly, they must recognize that politics is a key cause of economic inequality. And since most developing countries receive little foreign investment, the wealthy nations must also acknowledge that the "Washington consensus," which assumes that free markets will bring about economic convergence, is mistaken. If they at least admit these realities, they will abandon the notion that their own particular strategies are the best for all countries. In turn, they should allow poorer countries considerable freedom to tailor development strategies to their own circumstances. In this more pragmatic view, the role of the state becomes pivotal.

Why have economists and policymakers not come to these conclusions sooner? Since the barriers erected by rich countries are seen as vital to political stability, leaders of those countries find it convenient to overlook them and focus instead on the part of the global economy that has been liberalized. The rich countries' political power in multilateral organizations makes it difficult for developing nations to challenge this self-serving world-view. And standard academic solutions may do as much harm as good, given their focus on economic stability and growth rather than on the institutions that underpin markets. Economic theory has ignored the political issues at stake in modernizing institutions, incorrectly assuming that market-based prices can allocate resources appropriately.

The fiasco of reform in Russia has forced a belated reappraisal of this blind trust in markets. Many observers now admit that the transition economies needed appropriate property rights and an effective state to enforce those rights as much as they needed the liberalization of prices. Indeed, liberalization without property rights turned out to be the path to gangsterism, not capitalism. China, with a more effective state, achieved much greater success in its transition than did Russia, even though Beijing proceeded much more slowly with liberalization and privatization.

Economic development requires the transformation of institutions as well as the freeing of prices, which in turn requires political and social modernization as well as economic reform. The state plays a key role in this process; without it, developmental strategies have little hope of succeeding. The creation of effective states in the developing world will not be driven by familiar market forces, even if pressures from capital markets can force fiscal and monetary discipline. And in a world still governed by "states rights," real progress in achieving accountable governments will require reforms beyond the mandates of multilateral institutions.

2.2. GO WITH THE FLOW

IN THEORY, globalization provides an opportunity to raise incomes through increased specialization and trade. This opportunity is conditioned by the size of the markets in question, which in turn depends on geography, transportation costs, communication networks, and the institutions that underpin markets. Free trade increases both the size of the market and the pressure to improve economic performance. Those who are most competitive take advantage of the enhanced market opportunities to survive and prosper.

Neoclassical economic theory predicts that poor countries should grow faster than rich ones in a free global market. Capital from rich nations in search of cheaper labor should flow to poorer economies, and labor should migrate from low-income areas toward those with higher wages. As a result, labor and capital costs -and eventually income -in rich and poor areas should eventually converge.

The U.S. economy demonstrates how this theory can work in a free market with the appropriate institutions. Since the i88os, a remarkable convergence of incomes among the country's regions has occurred. The European Union has witnessed a similar phenomenon, with the exceptions of Greece and Italy's southern half, the Mezzogiorno. What is important, however, is that both America and the Eu enjoy labor and capital mobility as well as free internal trade.

But the rest of the world does not fit this pattern. The most recent World Development Report shows that real per capita incomes for the richest one-third of countries rose by an annual 1.9 percent between 1970 and 1995, whereas the middle third went up by only 0.7 percent and the bottom third showed no increase at all. In the Western industrial nations and Japan alone, average real incomes have been rising about 2.5 percent annually since 1950-a fact that further accentuates the divergence of global income. These rich countries account for about 60 percent of world GDP but only 15 percent of world population.

Why is it that the poor countries continue to fall further behind? One key reason is that most rich countries have largely excluded the international flow of labor into their markets since the interwar period. As a result, low-skilled labor is not free to flow across international boundaries in search of more lucrative jobs. From an American or European perspective, immigration appears to have risen in recent years, even approaching its previous peak of a century ago in the United States. Although true, this comparison misses the central point. Billions of poor people could improve their standard of living by migrating to rich countries. But in 1997, the United States allowed in only 737,000 immigrants from developing nations, while Europe admitted about 665,000. Taken together, these flows are only 0.04 percent of all potential immigrants.

The point is not that the rich countries should permit unfettered immigration. A huge influx of cheap labor would no doubt be politically explosive; many European countries have already curtailed immigration from poor countries for fear of a severe backlash. But the more salient issue is that rich nations who laud liberalism and free markets are rejecting those very principles when they restrict freedom of movement. The same goes for agricultural imports. Both Europe and Japan have high trade barriers in agriculture, while the United States remains modestly protectionist.

Mainstream economic theory does provide a partial rationalization for rich-country protectionism: Immigration barriers need not be a major handicap to poor nations because they can be offset by capital flows from industrialized economies to developing ones. In other words, poor people need not demand space in rich countries because the rich will send their capital to help develop the poor countries. This was indeed the case before World War I, but it has not been so since World War II.

But the question of direct investment, which typically brings technologies and know -how as well as financial capital, is more complicated than theories would predict. The total stock of foreign direct investment did rise almost sevenfold from 1980 to 1997, increasing from 4 percent to 12 percent of world GDP during that period. But very little has gone to the poorest countries. In 1997, about 70 percent went from one rich country to another, 8 developing countries received about 20 percent, and the remainder was divided among more than 100 poor nations. According to the World Bank, the truly poor countries received less than 7 percent of the foreign direct investment to all developing countries in 1992-98. At the same time, the unrestricted opening of capital markets in developing countries gives larger firms from rich countries the opportunity for takeovers that are reminiscent of colonialism. It is not accidental that rich countries insist on open markets where they have an advantage and barriers in agriculture and immigration, where they would be at a disadvantage.

As for the Asian "tigers," their strong growth is due largely to their high savings rate, not foreign capital. Singapore stands out because it has enjoyed a great deal of foreign investment, but it has also achieved one of the highest domestic-savings rates in the world, and its government has been a leading influence on the use of these funds. China is now repeating this pattern, with a savings rate of almost 40 percent Of GDP. This factor, along with domestic credit creation, has been its key motor of economic growth. China now holds more than $100 billion in low-yielding foreign -exchange reserves, the second largest reserves in the world.

In short, global markets offer opportunities for all, but opportunities do not guarantee results. Most poor countries have been unable to avail themselves of much foreign capital or to take advantage of increased market access. True, these countries have raised their trade ratios (exports plus imports) from about 35 percent of their GDP in 1981 to almost 50 percent in 1997. But without the Asian tigers, developing country exports remain less than 25 percent of world exports.

Part of the problem is that the traditional advantages of poor countries have been in primary commodities (agriculture and minerals), and these categories have shrunk from about 70 percent of world trade in 1900 to about 2o percent at the end of the century. Opportunities for growth in the world market have shifted from raw or semi-processed commodities toward manufactured goods and services-and, within these categories, toward more knowledge-intensive segments. This trend obviously favors rich countries over poor ones, since most of the latter are still peripheral players in the knowledge economy. (Again, the Asian tigers are the exception. In 1995, they exported as much in high technology goods as did France, Germany, Italy, and Britain combined -- which together have three times the population of the tigers.)

2.3. One Country, Two Systems

WHY is the performance of poor countries so uneven and out of sync with theoretical forecasts? Systemic barriers at home and abroad inhibit the economic potential of poorer nations, the most formidable of these obstacles being their own domestic political and administrative problems. These factors, of course, lie outside the framework of mainstream economic analysis. A useful analogy is the antebellum economy of the United States, which experienced a similar set of impediments.

Like today's "global village," the U.S. economy before the Civil War saw incomes diverge as the South fell behind the North. One reason for the Confederacy's secession and the resulting civil war was Southern recognition that it was falling behind in both economic and political power, while the richer and more populous North was attracting more immigrants. Half of the U.S. population lived in the North in 1780; by 1860, this share had climbed to two-thirds. In 1775, incomes in the five original Southern states equaled those in New England, even though wealth (including slaves) was disproportionately concentrated in the South. By 1840, incomes in the northeast were about 50 percent higher than those in the original Southern states; the North's railroad mileage was about 40 percent greater (and manufacturing investment four times higher)

than the South's. As the economist Robert Fogel has pointed out, the South was not poor-in 1860 it was richer than all European states except England-but Northern incomes were still much higher and increasing.

Why had Southern incomes diverged from those in the North under the same government, laws, and economy? Almost from their inception, the Southern colonies followed a different path from the North -specializing in plantation agriculture rather than small farms with diversified crops-due to geography and slavery. Thanks to slave labor, Southerners were gaining economies of scale and building comparative advantage in agriculture, exporting their goods to world markets and the North. Gang labor outproduced "free" (paid) labor. But the North was building even greater advantages by developing a middle class, a manufacturing sector, and a more modern social and political culture. With plans to complete transcontinental railroads pending, the North was on the verge of achieving economic and political dominance and the capacity to shut off further expansion of slavery in the West. The South chose war over Northern domination -and modernization.

Although the Constitution guaranteed free trade and free movement of capital and labor, the institution of slavery meant that the South had much less factor mobility than the North. It also ensured less development of its human resources, a less equal distribution of income, a smaller market for manufactures, and a less dynamic economy. It was less attractive to both European immigrants and external capital. With stagnant incomes in the older states, it was falling behind. In these respects, it was a forerunner of many of today's poor countries, especially those in Latin America.

What finally put the South on the path to economic convergence? Four years of civil war with a total of 600,000 deaths and vast destruction of property were only a start. Three constitutional amendments and twelve years of military "reconstruction" were designed to bring equal rights and due process to the South. But the reestablishment of racial segregation following Reconstruction led to sharecropping as former slaves refused to return to the work gangs. Labor productivity dropped so much that Southern incomes fell to about half of the North's in 1880. In fact, income convergence did not take off until the 1940s, when a wartime boom in the North's industrial cities attracted Southern migrants in search of better jobs. At the same time, the South began drawing capital as firms sought lower wages, an anti-union environment, and military contracts in important congressional districts. But this process did not fully succeed until the 1960s, as new federal laws and federal troops brought full civil rights to the South and ensured that the region could finally modernize.

2.4. The Great Divide

Although slavery is a rarity today, the traditional U.S. divide between North and South provides a good model for understanding contemporary circumstances in many developing countries. In the American South, voter intimidation, segregated housing, and very unequal schooling were the rule, not the exception-and such tactics are repeated today by the elites in today's poor countries. Brazil, Mexico, and Peru had abundant land relative to population when the Europeans arrived, and their incomes roughly approximated those in North America, at least until 1700. The economists Stanley Engerman and Kenneth Sokoloff have pointed out that these states, like the Confederacy, developed agricultural systems based on vast landholdings for the production of export crops such as sugar and coffee. Brazil and many Caribbean islands also adopted slavery, while Peru and Mexico relied on forced indigenous labor rather than African slaves.

History shows that the political development of North America and developing nations -most of which were colonized by Europeans at some point -was heavily influenced by mortality. In colonies with tolerable death rates (Australia, Canada, New Zealand, and the United States), the colonists soon exerted pressure for British-style protections of persons and property. But elsewhere (most of Africa, Latin America, Indonesia, and to a lesser degree, India), disease caused such high mortality rates that the few resident Europeans were permitted to exploit a disenfranchised laboring class, whether slave or free. When the colonial era ended in these regions, it was followed by "liberationist" regimes (often authoritarian and incompetent) that maintained the previous system of exploitation for the advantage of a small domestic elite. Existing inequalities within poor countries continued; policies and institutions rarely protected individual rights or private initiative for the bulk of the population and allowed elites to skim off rents from any sectors that could bear it. The economist Hernando de Soto has shown how governments in the developing world fail to recognize poor citizens' legal titles to their homes and businesses, thereby depriving them of the use of their assets for collateral. The losses in potential capital to these countries have dwarfed the cumulative capital inflows going to these economies in the last century.

The legacy of these colonial systems also tends to perpetuate the unequal distribution of income, wealth, and political power while limiting capital mobility. Thus major developing nations such as Brazil, China, India, Indonesia, and Mexico are experiencing a divergence of incomes by province within their economies, as labor and capital fail to find better opportunities. Even in recent times, local elites have fought to maintain oppressive conditions in Brazil, El Salvador, Guatemala, Mexico, Nicaragua, and Peru. Faced with violent intimidation, poor people in these countries have suffered from unjust law enforcement similar to what was once experienced by black sharecroppers in the American South.

Modernization and economic development inevitably threaten the existing distribution of power and income, and powerful elites continue to protect the status quo-even if it means that their society as a whole falls further behind. It takes more than a constitution, universal suffrage, and regular elections to achieve governmental accountability and the rule of law. It may well be that only the right of exit-emigration-can peacefully bring accountability to corrupt and repressive regimes. Unlike the U.S. federal government, multilateral institutions lack the legitimacy to intervene in the internal affairs of most countries. Europe's economic takeoff in the second half of the nineteenth century was aided by the emigration of 60 million people to

North America, Argentina, Brazil, and Australia. This emigration-- about 10 percent of the labor force -helped raise European wages while depressing inflated wages in labor-scarce areas such as Australia and the United States. A comparable out - migration of labor from today's poor countries would involve hundreds of millions of people.

Of course, Latin America has seen some success. Chile has received the most attention for its free market initiatives, but its reforms were implemented by a brutally repressive military regime -hardly a model for achieving economic reform through democratic processes. Costa Rica would seem to be a much better model for establishing accountability, but its economic performance has not been as striking as Chile's.

Italy, like the United States in an earlier era, is another good example of "one country, two systems." Italy's per capita income has largely caught up with that of its European neighbors over the past 20 years, even exceeding Britain's and equaling France's in 1990, but its Mezzogiorno has failed to keep up. Whereas overall Italian incomes have been converging toward those of the EU, Mezzogiorno incomes have been diverging from those in the north. Southern incomes fell from 65 percent of the northern average in 1975 to 56 percent 20 years later; in Calabria, they fell to 47 percent of the northern average. Southern unemployment rose from 8 percent in 1975 to 19 percent in 1995 -almost three times the northern average. In short, 50 years of subsidies from Rome and the EU have failed to stop the Mezzogiorno from falling further behind. Instead, they have yielded local regimes characterized by greatly increased public -sector employment, patronage, dependency, and corruption -not unlike the results of foreign aid for developing countries. And the continuing existence of the Mafia further challenges modernization.

Democracy, then, is not enough to ensure that the governed are allowed to reap the gains of their own efforts. An effective state requires good laws as well as law enforcement that is timely, evenhanded, and accessible to the poor. In many countries, achieving objective law enforcement means reducing the extralegal powers of vested interests. When this is not possible, the only recourse usually available is emigration. But if the educated elite manages to emigrate while the masses remain trapped in a society that is short of leaders, the latter will face even more formidable odds as they try to create effective institutions and policies. Although Italians still emigrate from south to north, the size of this flow is declining, thanks in part to generous transfer payments that allow them to consume almost as much as northerners. In addition, policymaking for the Mezzogiorno is still concentrated in Rome.

The immigration barriers in rich countries not only foreclose opportunities in the global village to billions of poor people, they help support repressive, pseudo democratic governments by denying the citizens of these countries the right to vote against the regime with their feet. In effect, the strict dictates of sovereignty allow wealthy nations to continue to set the rules in their own favor while allowing badly governed poor nations to continue to abuse their own citizens and retard economic development. Hence the remedy for income divergence must be political as well as economic.

2.5. Getting Institutions Right

According to Economic Theory, developing nations will create and modernize the institutions needed to underpin their markets so that their markets and firms can gradually match the performance of rich countries. But reality is much more complex than theory. For example, de Soto's analysis makes clear that effectively mobilizing domestic resources offers a much more potent source of capital for most developing nations than foreign inflows do. Yet mainstream economists and their formal models largely ignore these resources. Western economic advisers in Russia were similarly blindsided by their reliance on an economic model that had no institutional context and no historical perspective. Economists have scrambled in recent years to correct some of these shortcomings, and the Washington consensus now requires the "right" institutions as well as the "right" prices. But little useful theory exists to guide policy when it comes to institutional analysis, and gaps in the institutional foundations in most developing countries leave economic models pursuing unrealistic solutions or worse.

The adjustment of institutions inevitably favors certain actors and disadvantages others. As a result, modernization causes conflict that must be resolved through politics as well as economics. At a minimum, successful development signifies that the forces for institutional change have won out over the status quo. Achieving a "level playing field" signifies that regulatory and political competition is well governed.

Economists who suggest that all countries must adopt Western institutions to achieve Western levels of income often fail to consider the changes and political risks involved. The experts who recommended that formerly communist countries apply "shock therapy" to markets and democracy disregarded the political and regulatory issues involved. Each change requires a victory in the "legislative market" and successful persuasion within the state bureaucracy for political approval. Countries with lower incomes and fewer educated people than Russia face even more significant developmental challenges just to achieve economic stability, let alone attract foreign investment or make effective use of it. Institutional deficiencies, not capital shortages, are the major impediment to development, and as such they must be addressed before foreign investors will be willing to send in capital.

Although price liberalization can be undertaken rapidly, no rapid process (aside from revolution) exists for an economy modernizing its institutions. Boris Yeltsin may be credited with a remarkable turnover, if not a coup d'etat, but his erratic management style and the lack of parliamentary support ensured that his government would never be strong. In these circumstances, helping the new Russian regime improve law enforcement should have come ahead of mass privatization. Launching capitalism in a country where no one other than apparatchiks had access to significant amounts of capital was an open invitation to gangsterism and a discredited system. Naive economic models made for naive policy recommendations.

2.6. How the West Won

The State's crucial role is evident in the West's economic development. European economic supremacy was forged not by actors who followed a "Washington consensus" model but by strong states. In the fifteenth century, European incomes were not much higher than those in China, India, or Japan. The nation-state was a European innovation that replaced feudalism and established the rule of law; in turn, a legal framework was formed for effective markets. Once these countries were in the lead, they were able to continuously increase their edge through technological advances. In addition, European settlers took their civilization with them to North America and the South Pacific, rapidly raising these areas to rich -country status as well. Thus Europe's early lead became the basis for accumulating further advantages with far-reaching implications.

Europe's rise to economic leadership was not rapid at first. According to the economist Angus Maddison, Europe's economy grew around 0.07 percent a year until 1700; only after 1820 did it reach one percent. But the pace of technological and institutional innovation accelerated thereafter. Meanwhile, discovery of new markets in Africa, Asia, and the Americas created new economic opportunities. Secular political forces overthrew the hegemony of the Catholic Church. Feudalism was eroded by rising incomes and replaced by a system that financed government through taxes, freeing up land and labor to be traded in markets. Markets permitted a more efficient reallocation of land and labor, allowing further rises in incomes. Effective property rights allowed individuals to keep the fruits of their own labor, thereby encouraging additional work. And privatization of common land facilitated the clearing of additional acreage.

The nation -state helped forge all these improvements. It opened up markets by expanding territory; reduced transaction costs; standardized weights, measures, and monetary units; and cut transport costs by improving roads, harbors, and canals. In addition, it was the state that established effective property rights. The European state system thrived on flexible alliances, which constantly changed to maintain a balance of power. Military and economic rivalries prompted states to promote development in agriculture and commerce as well as technological innovation in areas such as shipping and weaponry.

Absent the hegemony of a single church or state, technology was diffused and secularized. Clocks, for instance, transferred timekeeping from the monastery to the village clock tower; the printing press did much the same for the production and distribution of books.

Europe's development contrasts sharply with Asia's. In the early modern era, China saw itself as the center of the world, without real rivals. It had a much larger population than Europe and a far bigger market as well. But though the Chinese pioneered the development of clocks, the printing press, gunpowder, and iron, they did not have the external competitive stimulus to promote economic development. Meanwhile, Japan sealed itself off from external influences for more than 200 years, while India, which had continuous competition within the subcontinent, never developed an effective national state prior to the colonial era.

The Europeans also led in establishing accountable government, even though it was achieved neither easily nor peacefully. Most European states developed the notion that the sovereign (whether a monarch or a parliament) had a duty to protect subjects and property in return for taxes and service in the army. Rulers in the Qing, Mughal, and Ottoman Empires, in contrast, never recognized a comparable responsibility to their subjects. During the middle Ages, Italy produced a number of quasi-democratic city -states, and in the seventeenth century Holland created the first modern republic after a century of rebellion and warfare with Spain. Britain achieved constitutional monarchy in 1689, following two revolutions. After a bloody revolution and then dictatorship, France achieved accountable government in the nineteenth century.

Europe led the way in separating church and state-an essential precursor to free inquiry and adoption of the scientific method-after the Thirty Years' War. The secular state in turn paved the way for capitalism and its "creative destruction." Creative destruction could hardly become the norm until organized religion lost its power to execute as heretics those entrepreneurs who would upset the status quo. After the Reformation, Europeans soon recognized another fundamental tenet of capitalism: the role of interest as a return for the use of capital. Capitalism required that political leaders allow private hands to hold power as well as wealth; in turn, power flowed from the rural nobility to merchants in cities. European states also permitted banks, insurance firms, and stock markets to develop. The "yeast" in this recipe lay in the notion that private as well as state organizations could mobilize and reallocate society's resources -an idea with profound social, political, and economic implications today.

Most of Europe's leading powers did not rely on private initiative alone but adopted mercantilism to promote their development. This strategy used state power to create a trading system that would raise national income, permitting the government to enhance its own power through additional taxes. Even though corruption was sometimes a side effect, the system generally worked well. Venice was the early leader, from about 1000 to 1500; the Dutch followed in the sixteenth and seventeenth centuries; Britain became dominant in the eighteenth century. In Britain, as in the other cases, mercantilist export promotion was associated with a dramatic rise in state spending and employment (especially in the navy), as well as "crony capitalism." After World War II, export-promotion regimes were adopted by Japan, South Korea, Singapore, and Taiwan with similar success. Today, of course, such strategies are condemned as violations of global trade rules, even for poor countries.

Finally, geography played a pivotal role in Europe's rise, providing a temperate climate, navigable rivers, accessible coastline, and defensible boundaries for future states. In addition, Europe lacked the conditions for the production of labor- intensive commodities such as coffee, cotton, sugar, or tobacco-production that might have induced the establishment of slavery. Like in the American North, European agriculture was largely rain -fed, diversified, and small-scale.

Europe's rise, then, was partly due to the creation and diffusion of technological innovations and the gradual accumulation of capital. But the underlying causes were political and social. The creation of the nation-state and institutionalized state rivalry fostered government accountability. Scientific enlightenment and upward social mobility, spurred by healthy competition, also helped Europe achieve such transformations. But many of today's developing countries still lack these factors crucial for economic transformation.

2.7. Playing Catch-Up

Globalization offers opportunities for all nations, but most developing countries are very poorly positioned to capitalize on them. Malarial climates, limited access to navigable water, long distances to major markets, and unchecked population growth are only part of the problem. Such countries also have very unequal income structures inherited from colonial regimes, and these patterns of income distribution are hard to change unless prompted by a major upheaval such as a war or a revolution. But as serious as these disadvantages are, the greatest disadvantage has been the poor quality of government.

If today's global opportunities are far greater and potentially more accessible than at any other time in world history, developing countries are also further behind than ever before. Realistic political logic suggests that weak governments need to show that they can manage their affairs much better before they pretend to have strategic ambitions. So what kind of catch-up models could they adopt?

Substituting domestic goods for imports was the most popular route to economic development prior to the 1980s. But its inward orientation made those who adopted it unable to take advantage of the new global opportunities and ultimately it led to a dead end. Although the United States enjoyed success with such a strategy from 1790 until 1940, no developing country has a home market large enough to support a modern economy today. The other successful early growth model was European mercantilism, namely export promotion, as pioneered by Venice, the Dutch republic, Britain, and Germany. Almost all of the East Asian success stories, China included, are modern versions of the export -oriented form of mercantilism.

For its part, free trade remains the right model for rich countries because it provides decentralized initiatives to search for tomorrow's market opportunities. But it does not necessarily promote development. Britain did not adopt free trade until the

1840s, long after it had become the world's leading industrial power. The prescription of lower trade barriers may help avoid even worse strategies at the hands of bad governments, but the Washington -consensus model remains best suited for those who are ahead rather than behind.

Today's shareholder capitalism brings additional threats to poor countries, first by elevating compensation for successful executives, and second by subordinating all activities to those that maximize shareholder value. Since 1970, the estimated earnings of an American chief executive have gone from 30 times to 450 times that of the average worker. In the leading developing countries, this ratio is still less than 50. Applying a similar "market-friendly" rise in executive compensation within the developing world would therefore only aggravate the income gap, providing new ammunition for populist politicians. In addition, shareholder capitalism calls for narrowing the managerial focus to the interests of shareholders, even if this means dropping activities that offset local market imperfections. A leading South African bank has shed almost a million small accounts -mostly held by blacks-to raise its earnings per share. Should this bank, like its American counterparts, have an obligation to serve its community, including its black members, in return for its banking license?

Poor nations must improve the effectiveness of their institutions and bureaucracies in spite of entrenched opposition and poorly paid civil servants. As the journalist Thomas Friedman has pointed out, it is true that foreign-exchange traders can dump the currencies of poorly managed countries, thereby helping discipline governments to restrain their fiscal deficits and lax monetary policies. But currency pressures will not influence the feudal systems in Pakistan and Saudi Arabia, the theocracies in Afghanistan and Iran, or the kleptocracies in Kenya or southern Mexico. The forces of capital markets will not restrain Brazilian squatters as they take possession of "public lands" or the slums of Rio de Janeiro or Sao Paulo, nor will they help discipline landlords and vigilantes in India's Bihar as they fight for control of their state. Only strong, accountable government can do that.

2.8. Looking Ahead

Increased trade and investment have indeed brought great improvements in some countries, but the global economy is hardly a win-win situation. Roughly one billion people earn less than $1 per day, and their numbers are growing. Economic resources to ameliorate such problems exist, but the political and administrative will to realize the potential of these resources in poor areas is lacking. Developing-nation governments need both the pressure to reform their administrations and institutions, and the access to help in doing so. But sovereignty removes much of the external pressure, while immigration barriers reduce key internal motivation. And the Washington consensus on the universality of the rich- country model is both simplistic and self-serving.

The world needs a more pragmatic, country-by -country approach, with room for neomercantilist regimes until such countries are firmly on the convergence track. Poor nations should be allowed to do what today's rich countries did to get ahead, not be forced to adopt the laissez-faire approach. Insisting on the merits of comparative advantage in low-wage, low-growth industries are a sure way to stay poor. And continued poverty will lead to rising levels of illegal immigration and low-level violence, such as kidnappings and vigilante justice, as the poor take the only options that remain. Over time, the rich countries will be forced to pay more attention to the fortunes of the poor-if only to enjoy their own prosperity and safety.

Still, the key initiatives must come from the poor countries, not the rich. In the last 50 years, China, India, and Indonesia have led the world in reducing poverty. In China, it took civil war and revolution, with tens of millions of deaths, to create a strong state and economic stability; a de facto coup d'etat in 1978 brought about a very fortunate change of management. The basic forces behind Chinese reform were political and domestic, and their success depended as much on better using resources as opening up markets. Meanwhile, the former Soviet Union and Africa lie at the other extreme. Their economic decline stems from their failure to maintain effective states and ensure the rule of law.

It will not be surprising if some of today's states experience failure and economic decline in the new century. Argentina, Colombia, Indonesia, and Pakistan will be obvious cases to watch, but other nations could also suffer from internal regional failures -for example, the Indian state of Bihar. Income growth depends heavily on the legal, adminsitrative, and political capabilities of public actors in sovereign states. That is why, in the end, external economic advice and aid must go beyond formal models and conform to each country's unique political and social context.

3. GLOBAL MARKETS AND THE GLOBAL VILLAGE IN THE 21ST CENTURY

It is almost 40 years since Marshall McLuhan coined the phrase "global village" in his book The Gutenberg Galaxy. He argued that electronic technology was shrinking the planet, that "Time has ceased and space has vanished".

That was not true then. CNN did not exist, nor did the internet, and the explosion of telephone communications was just beginning. Only a few years before McLuhan wrote, when the first telephone cables were laid across the Atlantic in 1956, they carried 36 simultaneous conversations. Today's fibre-optic counterparts carry no fewer than 10 million conversations.

No, time has not ceased and space has not vanished -- but life does seem to be moving rapidly that way. Taken together, telecommunications, satellites, computers and fibre-optics are halving the cost of processing, storing and transmitting information every 18 months. The global village even has its own market square in the shape of the internet -- a forum for commerce, information, entertainment and personal interaction that makes previously undreamed of access to information available almost instantly and at extraordinarily low cost. Estimates suggest that 250 million people around the world use the internet already, with the number rising every day. Today 40% of the world population has an internet connection, in 1995, it was less than 1%.The internet users has increased tenfold from 1999 to 2013. Now there are 3.5 billion people in the world.

Globalization is not only the internet and telecommunications; it is also the more traditional fare of economists: trade in goods; and trade in assets. The theoretical case for free trade is that it permits countries to concentrate on activities in which they enjoy comparative advantage and subjects firms to the healthy discipline of foreign competition. This means higher productivity and increased living standards, while consumers enjoy access to a wider variety of goods and services at lower cost. This is true not only in theory, it is true also in practice: our post-World War II prosperity is based in large part on the rapid expansion of international trade in goods and services, which year after year has grown more rapidly than production. The theoretical argument for the free movement of capital is essentially the same as the argument for free trade in goods: money can be channeled to its most profitable uses worldwide, financing productive investment opportunities even where domestic savings are scarce. However the recent crises have made that a more controversial proposition.

Globalization can create losers as well as winners. And it is human nature that those who lose will be more vocal than those who gain. Free trade prompts fears that competition from low wage economies will displace workers from well-paid factory jobs into less attractive service sector work -- a process that Europeans tend to see in terms of McDonald's, but which applies also to the shift of employment towards high tech industries. Globalization is also seen as a constraint on national economic policies. Huge swings in capital flows have been associated with severe financial crises and economic disruptions in a succession of previously rapidly growing emerging market economies. And there are other concerns, particularly over cultural homogenization, with some intellectuals around the world despairing at what they see as the vulgarizing influence of Hollywood movies and Disney theme parks.

3.1. Global capital markets

By their nature capital flows will never be entirely smooth or predictable. But as the recessions in several East Asian countries demonstrated last year, the volatility of capital flows has been excessive. It has subjected recipient countries to crises that are bigger and more frequent than they need to be. The way in which Russia's devaluation and unilateral debt restructuring saw the crisis leap to Latin America also indicates that there is too much contagion in the system. To address these problems, actions are required: from governments and the private sector in emerging markets; from governments and the private sector in capital exporting nations; and from the international institutions themselves.

For the emerging market countries, as for all countries, prudent macroeconomic policy is a prerequisite. Sound public finances and the pursuit of low inflation are hardly controversial recommendations, although they are easier to prescribe than to pursue. More controversial is a country's choice of exchange rate regime, a topic over which economists have argued for a century without reaching any firm conclusion. But it is surely no coincidence that the countries that experienced the major external crises of the last two-and-a-half years -- Thailand, Korea, Indonesia, Russia and Brazil -- all had fixed or essentially pegged exchange rates. Countries with more flexible arrangements -- including Mexico in 1998, South Africa and Turkey -- also suffered, but to nothing like the same degree. So most countries with open capital accounts are now more likely to choose flexible regimes. If they fix, they may well emulate Hong Kong or Argentina and do so definitively through a currency board. The currency board regimes have withstood the recent hostile fire.

What about using controls to moderate capital inflows and outflows? There is no good reason to restrain inflows of long-term capital, especially of foreign direct investment. But recent experience suggests a stronger case for market-based controls (like those adopted by Chile) to restrain potentially destabilizing inflows of short-term capital. It may be tempting to impose controls on capital outflows in response to short-term problems, as Malaysia did last year, but the longer term consequences are likely to be adverse, and indeed Malaysia has gradually removed some of the controls imposed in 1998. Experience in Latin America during the 1980s showed that controls of this sort tend to be inefficient, widely circumscribed and a barrier to future borrowing. It is surely significant that policymakers in the region have chosen not to travel this road again.

Weak banking and financial systems have been at the center of most recent crises, and they need to be strengthened. This has been a key objective in IMF-supported programs in the Asian crisis countries. It is also an increasingly important focus of our work in other member countries of the IMF. As the Basle

Committee's Core Principles make clear, the ingredients of a strong banking system include good bankers, strong supervision and healthy competition, especially from foreign institutions. Emerging market countries also need to strengthen corporate governance and finance, adopting appropriate auditing and accounting standards and rigorously enforcing bankruptcy laws.

The countries from which capital flows originate also have their part to play. Global prosperity is impossible if the industrialized countries that produce two-thirds of world output are not prospering. So they must pursue policies to achieve sustained growth with low inflation. Fortunately, around the world most recent growth surprises have been favorable, and growth looks as though it will be significantly better than forecast just a few months ago. In addition, the industrialized countries can take further steps to try to stabilize capital flows originating in their countries, for example by supporting the conclusions of the Financial Stability Forum studies on highly leveraged institutions and offshore financial centers now in progress. One important contribution will be the reform of the Basle capital adequacy standards, which in the past have made short-term bank loans more profitable relative to long-term ones.

While the responsibility for implementing these measures lies ultimately with the emerging market and industrial countries themselves, international organizations have an important role in encouraging and helping them to do so. The international community has placed particular emphasis on the development of international standards and principles. Those completed or in the pipeline cover banking supervision, securities market regulation, accounting, auditing, corporate governance, fiscal transparency, statistical dissemination and the transparency of monetary and financial policies. Of these, the IMF has been responsible for the development of statistical standards, and those for the transparency of fiscal policy, and of monetary and financial policies.

Monitoring of how well countries are implementing these standards will be undertaken mostly in the context of regular IMF surveillance, drawing on the assistance of relevant experts. Together with our colleagues in the World Bank, IMF experts are also beginning to carry out FSSAs -- Financial Sector

Stability Assessments -- to help countries identify the weaknesses in their financial system and repair them.

As an additional part of the international effort to strengthen financial systems, the Financial Stability Forum was established. It brings together officials from G7 finance ministries, central banks and financial sector supervisory bodies, as well as representatives of the international supervisors, the BIS, the IMF and World Bank. By bringing all these bodies together for the first time, it should be possible to improve coordination between them.

The IMF is also endeavoring to reduce the risk and cost of financial crises by strengthening its surveillance of national economic developments and policies, as well as the world economy and global capital markets. IMF are paying closer attention to capital account and financial sector issues, the sustainability of exchange rate regimes, debt and reserve management practices, vulnerability analyses, international aspects of a country's macroeconomic policies, cross-country comparisons and regional developments.

National authorities are also being given greater incentives to heed the advice they receive. Governments are encouraged to publish the executive board's annual Article IV assessment of their economy and policies. A pilot project has been set up allowing countries to publish the staff reports that underlie the surveillance process -- and Germany has just published its Article IV report for the first time.

The IMF is also encouraging sound policies by offering Contingent Credit Lines (CCLs) to countries that feel threatened by the sort of contagion that saw the recent crises spread so widely. But these will only be available to countries that have good policies, that are attempting to meet relevant international standards, that manage their external debt sensibly and that are pursing credit lines from private sector lenders.

The most difficult element in the reform of the international system, on which IMF are still working, is that of private sector involvement in the solution of financial crises. The official sector cannot allow the private sector to believe that its investments in emerging market countries carry an implicit official guarantee, and the only way that can be done is to make sure that the private sector plays its appropriate share in financing the resolution of crises. The issue of private sector involvement is currently to the fore in IMF programs with several countries, Ukraine, Pakistan, Romania and Ecuador. The circumstances of each country are different, and IMF are evolving towards a new strategy. The general outline is clear: there will be occasions, for instance if a country has become excessively indebted, has not been well managed, and requires very large scale public sector assistance, that the public sector will not provide enough financing to enable it to service all its debt. The country will then have to seek an arrangement with its private sector creditors to reduce its current debt service burden, for instance by restructuring the debt. For the country to receive public sector support in these circumstances, it will have to be implementing a program of macroeconomic stabilization and seeking a cooperative solution with its creditors -- the principle that contracts should whenever possible be honored, is essential to the efficient operation of the international financial system.

These measures -- greater transparency, standards and their monitoring, the emphasis on strengthening domestic policies and financial institutions, greater private sector involvement -- are a large part of the what has become known as the reform of the architecture of the international financial system. They are focused on the 30 or 40 emerging market economies that enjoy access to global capital markets, with all the risks and rewards that this implies. Some of these reforms are needed also in the advanced countries, and most are needed too in the other developing countries -- those yet to emerge fully into the international capital markets, but all of whom are engaged in international trade.

3.2. Trade

The free trade agenda is very much before us. Representatives of the 159 member countries of the World Trade Organization will meet in Seattle later this month to begin a fresh round of negotiations aimed at further opening of markets for goods, services and agricultural products. Success would bring valuable benefits. As mentioned earlier, trade has been one of the main engines of world growth since the end of World War II. And that is not just rhetoric. Every country that has grown fast in the post-War period has done so through a strategy of integration with the world economy, through rapidly growing exports and the accompanying imports. Germany knows that, so does Europe, so does Japan and East Asia. IMF must enable other countries to benefit in the same way.

But trade liberalization is not without vocal critics, many of whom will be protesting on the sidewalks of Seattle. Some objectors argue that free trade damages the environment. They point, for example, to the degradation of Mexico's industrial border region, where foreign investment stimulated by NAFTA has been accompanied by inadequate attention to wastewater treatment and the disposal of hazardous waste. Trade growth affects the environment through several channels. On the negative side, it tends to increase the scale of economic activity, which might be expected to imply more wear and tear on the environment. But the relationship is not a linear one. The incidence of many pollutants increases to begin with as incomes rise, only to fall again once living standards pass a given threshold.

Trade growth will also affect the environment when it prompts changes in the composition of economic activity, for example shifting the balance between heavy manufacturing and less polluting service sector outputs. Trade growth may also induce technological innovations that increase profitability and reduce environmental damage simultaneously, for example by using energy more efficiently. Consumers may also be prepared to pay more for products and services that they perceive to be friendly to the environment. In most countries these influences all play out in the context of increasingly stringent government regulations.

The net effect of trade on the environment is therefore ambiguous, depending in large part on the industry, country or pollutant involved. But in many cases the spillover effects of economic activity on the environment clearly do not respect national borders. The challenge for the international community is therefore to develop rules and incentives that accomplish legitimate environmental objectives without incurring excessive economic costs. IMF should support such measures, but at the same time IMF should be wary of essentially protectionist measures in the guise of environmental regulations.

Another concern raised by the trade liberalization agenda centers around the labor standards. Some argue that trade agreements -- or possibly the conditions that the IMF applies to its loans -- should require the observance of core labor standards. As enshrined in the various Conventions and Recommendations of the International Labor Organization, these standards include the right to organize into trade unions and bargain collectively, the right to equal pay and treatment for equal work, as well as the abolition of forced and child labor. The fear is that opening markets to countries that do not observe these standards may result in a "race to the bottom" in labor standards worldwide as businesses struggle to maintain market share against competitors who can exploit their workers to reduce costs.

The core standards form a set of principles with which most reasonable people would find it easy to agree. But as with environmental regulation, IMF should be wary of measures that disguise protectionism behind apparently noble motives. Interestingly, the evidence suggests that countries have little incentive to see their workers exploited. Recent studies by Dani Rodrik suggest there is no statistically significant relationship between a country's observance of core labor standards and its trade performance. Neither do weak labor standards encourage foreign direct investment by companies seeking workers to exploit.

Well-treated workers are generally more productive than exploited ones. So as long as competition forces companies to be as efficient as possible, strong labor standards should emerge naturally through enlightened self-interest. Will Martin, at the World Bank, and Keith Maskus, at the University of Colorado at Boulder, argued recently that this process characterized policy change in the US and Western Europe in the first half of this century and in Japan and Korea more recently. Erecting trade barriers to punish countries with poor labor standards could be a blunt instrument that worsens the problem at which it is aimed.

A free and open trading system can make a powerful contribution to the welfare of poorer nations. There is plenty of evidence -- and strong evidence -- that countries which are open to trade and investment grow more rapidly over time than those which shut them out of the global economy. Openness facilitates specialization and gives countries access to best practice technologies. But if less developed countries are to make the most of their participation in the global economy, then they need greater access to the markets of richer nations as well. IMF should all hope that the discussions getting under way in Seattle this month will help to achieve just that. And IMF should also work towards that end.

3.3. Development

To spread the benefits of globalization more widely, IMF must learn from past experience what works and what does not when it comes to promoting development and poverty reduction. Just as importantly, IMF must ensure that the international organizations work effectively together in supporting the strategies that countries choose to adopt. Support rather than leadership is the key. For IMF know that development strategies are more successful when they are "owned" by the countries directly concerned rather than imposed from outside.

From the perspective of the IMF, sound macroeconomic policies and market-oriented structural reforms have a vital contribution to make. There should be no doubt now that price stability, fiscal discipline and structural reform promote economic growth. And growth is the single most important factor that contributes to poverty reduction. Low inflation helps foster greater equality of incomes. And structural policies that ease factor and product market rigidities increase both the supply of essential goods and their availability to the poor.

But IMF have recognized increasingly that growth itself is not enough, and that the cause of poverty reduction and development in poor countries can be significantly advanced by policies directed at reducing poverty. Market reforms should be accompanied by the creation and maintenance of adequate social safety nets, for example, to limit the impact of necessary adjustment on the most vulnerable. And where fiscal retrenchment is necessary to stabilize the economy, IMF should do what they can to protect spending on the efficient provision of health, education and other social services. Growth-oriented economic policies and investments in social and human capital can be mutually reinforcing. Higher levels of economic activity reduce the costs of social dislocation and increase the revenues that governments have to spend on social goals. Investing in a healthier and better educated workforce can in turn promote higher productivity and stronger income growth.

While there is broad agreement on the policies that promote economic development, there is more debate about the speed at which they should be introduced. The experience of the transition economies is a case in point. As in other countries, anti-inflation policies and structural reforms were beneficial for growth. Some policies seem to have been more effective than others, with price liberalization and small-scale privatizations proving especially important. As for speed, the lesson of experience is that reforming quickly and comprehensively is more effective than doing so slowly and in piecemeal fashion. The boldest reformers have tended to be those countries closest to Western Europe, which spent the shortest periods under communism and which were economically most advanced when they fell under Soviet control or began transition.

With the 2017 approaching, the international community has given special attention to the difficulties faced by highly-indebted poor countries, many of which are in Africa. In 1996 that IMF and World Bank launched an initiative to reduce the external debt burdens of countries with good policies to levels that could be serviced sustainably through export earnings, aid and capital inflows. By removing the overhang of unsustainable debt it was hoped to encourage investment, thereby promoting economic growth and reducing poverty. The experience of the first countries to benefit showed that our initial estimates of sustainability were too conservative to achieve their objectives. There has also been greater recognition that debt relief should do more to free resources from government budgets to pay for essential social needs. So the initiative is being expanded, increasing the number of countries likely to benefit from 29 to 36 and at least doubling the relief available to a present value of $27b.

Up to now the IMF has contributed to this initiative through the Enhanced Structural Adjustment Facility (ESAF), our subsidized loan window for the poorest nations. This has now been reformed and renamed as the Poverty Reduction and Growth Facility. The change is not a cosmetic one. It reflects greater recognition of the complementary among macroeconomic, structural and social policies. This recognition is also being reflected in a more systematic framework for our cooperation with the World Bank in these countries, with the World Bank expected to take the lead in helping countries design and implement structural and anti-poverty programs.

Among policies to reduce poverty, access to credit can be very important. Many who are left behind by globalization lack the opportunity to borrow and invest in their own livelihoods. One powerful tool for helping in that regard is microcredit. These schemes lend relatively small sums to people who would otherwise be unable to borrow, and this is an area in which the World Bank has contributed a great deal of assistance. A survey carried out in April this year had responses from 925 microcredit practitioners with more than 22 million clients.

Microcredit is already addressing the disparity in access to communications I referred to earlier. Cellular telephones are a more efficient alternative to conventional networks in many developing countries. So in Bangladesh the Grameen Bank offered women loans of $350 to buy a telephone and pay for connection and training. These "wireless women" were then able to make a living as local service providers in rural areas. Providing women with access to credit has been an important objective of microcredit schemes, as experience suggests they are a good credit risk and that their earnings benefit other family members more than those of men. Microcredit has potential in many sectors. In Ghana, for example, many crop yields could be trebled if access to credit allowed smallholders to exploit available technology.

3.4. Are we prepared?

In the last decade, the Bretton Woods twins, the IMF and the World Bank, have made major adaptions in their organizations, the focus of their activities, and the ways in which they interact with member countries and the public. And this was also the decade in which the late-born third member of the global international organizations, the WTO, was born.

Across a broad variety of areas one believes that IMF are ready and willing to confront the challenges of the next century. The IMF are often accused of operating in a world very different than the one for which they were originally designed. But that -- the power to adapt -- is precisely what is most needed as IMF enter the coming century. For they can be sure that the new century will bring many unexpected challenges. Here again IMF have reason to be hopeful. In dealing with the problems of the poorest nations and with the fallout from the capital market volatility of recent years, the institutions have shown themselves willing and able to be flexible in the light of changing circumstances and a growing understanding of the problems IMF face.

This flexibility will be essential. When he developed the concept of the global village, McLuhan recognized that it would require all of us to be aware of the impact that our actions have beyond our national borders. "Electric speed at bringing all social and political functions together in a sudden implosion has heightened human awareness of responsibility to an intense degree", as he put it.

3.5. The Greek Crisis

When Greece joined the euro in 2001, confidence in the Greek economy grew and a big economic boom followed. But after the 2008 financial crisis, everything changed. Every country in Europe entered a recession, but because Greece was one of the poorest and most indebted countries, it suffered the most. The unemployment rate reached 28 percent in 2013, worse than the United States suffered during the Great Depression.

If Greece wasn't in the euro, it could have boosted its economy by printing more of its currency, the drachma. This would have lowered the value of the drachma in international markets, making Greek exports more competitive. It would also lower domestic interest rates, encouraging domestic investment and making it easier for Greek debtors to service their debts.

But Greece shares its monetary policy with the rest of Europe. And the German-dominated European Central Bank has given Europe a monetary policy that's about right for Germany, but so tight that it has thrust Greece into a depression.

So Greece is squeezed between a crushing debt burden — 179 percent of GDP, in 2016 about twice the level in the United States — and a deep depression that makes it difficult to raise the money it needs to make its debt payments. For the last five years, Greece has been negotiating with European Commission, the European Central Bank, and the International Monetary Fund (dubbed "the Troika") for financial assistance with its debt burden. Since 2010, the Troika has been providing Greece with loans in exchange for tax hikes and spending cuts.

Rich European nations such as Germany believe they're simply insisting that Greece live within its means. But the austere terms of the bailouts have caused resentment among Greeks and contributed to crisis-level unemployment and poverty. Greece elected a new left-wing prime minister, Alexis Tsipras, who promised to reject the previous bailout deal and secure a more favorable agreement.

But he has very little leverage. In 2010, Greek debt was widely held by private banks, so a Greek default could trigger a financial panic. But since then, this debt has been consolidated in the hands of rich European governments, greatly reducing the risk of a financial crisis if Greece defaults. So Greece faces a hard choice: it can accept the Troika's demands for further austerity. Or it can defy the Troika, which would likely lead to a default on Greek debt and possibly a Greek exit from the euro. The Greek government is holding a referendum on July 5 to let voters choose between these bad options.

In the meantime, the Greek economy is melting down. Knowing that Greek euro deposits could soon be transformed into devalued drachma deposits, Greek people have been rushing to ATMs to withdraw as much cash as they can. That has forced the Greek government to close the banks and limit withdrawals to €60 per day.

3.6. What's the latest?

Greece got the green light for the next round of bailout aid, money that will allow the country to keep paying its bills in the coming months. It also won additional pledges of debt relief, helping to ease concerns about another crisis in Greece at a time when Europe is dealing with an influx of migrants and a continuing terrorist threat.

Debt relief has been a contentious issue for creditors, with the International Monetary Fund and Germany lining up on opposite sides. The I.M.F. has insisted that

Greece cannot meet its budget goals without easing its debts, while Germany remains skeptical of cutting Athens more slack. They have reached a compromise, of sorts. Greece's creditors committed to debt relief, although not until 2018 at the earliest, provided the country continues to carry out painful changes.

3.7. How does the crisis affect the global financial system?

In the European Union, most real decision-making power, particularly on matters involving politically delicate things like money and migrants, rests with 28 national governments, each one beholden to its voters and taxpayers. This tension has grown only more acute since the January 1999 introduction of the euro, which binds 19 nations into a single currency zone watched over by the European Central Bank but leaves budget and tax policy in the hands of each country, an arrangement that some economists believe was doomed from the start.

Since Greece's debt crisis began in 2010, most international banks and foreign investors have sold their Greek bonds and other holdings, so they are no longer vulnerable to what happens in Greece. (Some private investors who subsequently plowed back into Greek bonds, betting on a comeback, regret that decision.) And in the meantime, the other crisis countries in the eurozone, like Portugal, Ireland and Spain, have taken steps to overhaul their economies and are much less vulnerable to market contagion than they were a few years ago.

3.8. What if Greece left the eurozone?

At the height of the debt crisis a few years ago, many experts worried that Greece's problems would spill over to the rest of the world. If Greece defaulted on its debt and exited the eurozone, they argued, it might create global financial shocks bigger than the collapse of Lehman Brothers did. Now, however, some people believe that if Greece were to leave the currency union, in what is known as a "Grexit," it would not be such a catastrophe. Europe has put up safeguards to limit the so-called financial contagion, in an effort to keep the problems from spreading to other countries. Greece, just a tiny part of the eurozone economy, could regain financial autonomy by leaving, these people contend — and the eurozone would actually be better off without a country that seems to constantly need its neighbors' support.

Greece does hold some leverage, however. European leaders are keen to avoid a new Greek crisis before a British referendum on membership to the European Union in June, and will most likely need Greece's help in tackling the Continent's continuing migration crisis, which has been concentrated in the Aegean Sea.

3.9. If Greece has received billions in bailouts, why has there still been a crisis?

The money was supposed to buy Greece time to stabilize its finances and quell market fears that the euro union itself could break up. While it has helped, Greece's economic problems have not gone away. The economy has shrunk by a quarter in five years, and unemployment is about 23 percent in 2016. The bailout money mainly goes toward paying off Greece's international loans, rather than making its way into the economy. And the government still has a staggering debt load that it cannot begin to pay down unless a recovery takes hold.

The government will now need to continue putting in place deep economic overhauls required by the bailout deal Prime Minister Alexis Tsipras brokered in August, as well as the unwinding of capital controls introduced after political upheaval prompted a run on Greek banks.

Greece's relations with Europe are in a fragile state, and several of its leaders are showing impatience, unlikely to tolerate the foot-dragging of past administrations. Under the terms of the bailout, Greece must continue to pass deep-reaching overhauls, many of them measures that were supposed to have been passed years ago.

4. THE GLOBAL VILLAGE AND THE SOCIAL AND CULTURAL ASPECTS OF GLOBALIZATION

4.1. Introduction

During the last few decades, human dynamics, institutional change, political relations and the global environment have become successively more intertwined. While increased global economic integration, global forms of governance, globally inter-linked social and environmental developments are often referred to as globalization, there is no unanimously-agreed upon definition of globalization. It means different things to different people. Depending on the researcher or commentator, it can mean the growing integration of markets and nation-states and the spread of technological advancements

(Friedman 1999); receding geographical constraints on social and cultural arrangements (Waters 1995); the increased dissemination of ideas and technologies (Albrow 1996); the threat to national sovereignty by trans-national actors (Beck 2000); or the transformation of the economic, political and cultural foundations of societies (Mittleman 2000). (Scholte 2002) argues for the globalization concept moving beyond being a buzzword for almost anything that is vaguely associated with it. Otherwise, discourse on globalization runs the risk of being brushed aside as being "... 'globaloney', 'global babble' and 'glob- blah-blah'".

If things were not sufficiently confusing, there has also been a spawning of preferred terms and descriptors. (Keohane and Nye 2000) distinguish between globalization and globalism, where the former term refers to the process by which globalism, i.e., "the networks of interdependence at multicontinental distances", is altered. The concept of internationalization is also highly significant (see, e.g., (Sassen 1993); (Chomsky 1994); (Held, McGrew et al. 1999). It refers to the role of the nation-state, often in cooperation and interaction with other nation-states, in adapting to global challenges.

In contrast, globalization is often thought to be a direct threat to the existence of the nation-state itself. So, by and large, internationalization is best thought of as the response to globalization.

The world increasingly shares problems and challenges that are not confined within national boundaries. Multi-regional financial crises, world-wide pandemics and cross-border pollution are obvious examples.

Such problems place the spotlight on the world's most prominent supra-national organizations – the United Nations (UN), the World Bank, the World Trade Organization (WTO) and the International Monetary Fund (IMF). Citizens' interests and welfare are increasingly being affected and, according to some, undermined by these bodies. If true, not only might such a development threaten representative democracy, but also it potentially abrogates the role of the nation-state itself.

It is also clear that globalization is something more than a purely economic phenomenon manifesting itself on a global scale. (Friedman 1999) associates modern-day globalization with Americanization (or more pointedly, U.S.-isation). And, after all, shouldn't everyone just flow with the times and spell globalization with a 'z'!? (Fiss and Hirsch 2005) analyses full-text datasets of newspaper articles and press releases related to globalization and show that the globalization discourse emerged as a response to greater U.S. involvement in the international economy. Between 1985 and 1998, the use of the term "globalization" increased substantially. The authors argue that the term originates in the early 1970s, with little consensus of what it means or how it should be defined. Politically, socially and culturally, globalization is thought to erode national cultures due to the pervasiveness of the global media and the information and communication technologies (ICT) revolution. The economic dimensions of globalization have an impact. The flows of goods and services and factors of production – labor and capital – have both direct and indirect effects on the nation-state (Gaston and Nelson 2004). With respect to the latter, national policies are affected – internationalization, recall – and the economic, political and socio-cultural fabric of societies is fundamentally altered.

Among the more visible manifestations of globalization are the greater international movement of goods and services, financial capital, information and people. In addition, there are technological developments, new and enhanced legal systems and institutions that facilitate these flows. On the cultural front, there are more international cultural exchanges, the spread of multi-culturalism and greater cultural diversity within many countries. Such developments are facilitated by the freer trade of more differentiated products as well as by tourism and immigration. Flows of immigration – both legal and illegal – also contribute to today's melting pot societies.

For many commentators, particularly economists, there is little doubt that globalization has produced significant gains at the global level (Bhagwati 2004). Foreign trade in goods and services, capital, technology and labor all move more freely across borders. In addition to economic gains, there have been significant benefits in the areas of culture and governance (Falk 2000). Public awareness of issues such as human rights, democracy and gender equality has increased significantly because of the greater access to newspapers, radio, television, telephones, computers and the internet. These developments have arguably led to improved allocative efficiency that, in turn, enhances growth and human development (UNDP 1999).

At the same time, globalization is also perceived as creating new threats: to individuals, societies and eco-systems. There are fears that it may exacerbate the gap between rich and poor – both within and across countries – creating new threats to human security in terms of financial volatility, political and cultural insecurity and environmental degradation. In other words, the beneficial, innovative and dynamic aspects of globalization are being tempered, and according to some more than offset, by forces that create disruption and marginalization, such as population growth and migration, the emergence of infectious diseases, widening disparities in development world-wide, climate change, an accelerating loss of bio-diversity and the scarcity and pollution of fresh-water resources.

The subject of fierce debate, protests and occasional violent confrontations, modern globalization is a lightning rod for both its supporters and detractors. The massive protests against globalization were highly visible at the WTO summit in Seattle in December 1999. Seattle became a launch pad for further protests whenever the WTO, World Bank, the Group of Eight (G-8) or multinationals convened, e.g., at Quebec, Geneva, Göteborg and Genoa. Although the anti-globalization activists were initially portrayed as a bunch of spoiled brats – donning New York Yankees baseball caps while chomping on Big Macs and quaffing Starbucks' lattes – there has been a growing acceptance that the protest movement is heterogeneous. It consists of various groups of people that do not all share the same vision. Some

oppose globalization in its current form because it is seen as predominantly capitalist in nature. Others see it as a threat to national sovereignty. Other groups do not oppose capitalism per se, but criticize the inability to more equitably distribute the benefits of globalization.

The delicate balance between the costs and benefits of greater global integration and reduced geographic isolation is illustrated by the temptation to closely associate contemporary globalization with the growth of terrorism. Terrorist attacks more often take place in foreign countries that are geographically, culturally, socially and politically distinct from the terrorists' own countries. On the other hand, the least globalized countries seem to suffer the worst of the significant terror attacks (Foreign Policy (with A.T. Kearney) 2005). This is but one of many issues, which seem so closely linked with the process of globalization.

4.2. The Global Village

The late 1960s witnessed remarkable socio-cultural changes. The rise of the flower power generation, anti-Vietnam protests, the sexual revolution, and movements for the emancipation of women, non- whites, homosexuals and other "minorities" represent only the tip of the iceberg. For example, the emergence of pop art also marked the change to a post-modern culture (Harvey 1989). Moreover, the publication of Marshall McLuhan's The Medium is the Massage in 1967, in which the world is described as becoming a 'global village', is one of the first socio-cultural landmarks that points at the existence of globalization. Considering these circumstances, it is impossible to regard globalization as purely an economic, political or technological phenomenon.

The increased influence of the media on our daily lives has not only changed our way of perceiving the world and our consumption patterns, it has also affected local cultures. In the view of the cultural pessimists, the United States (particularly Hollywood) has established a global culture, arguably at the cost of traditional and local ones (Bourdieu 1998). Youth the world over have especially embraced this culture, emphasizing the freedom of choice that this global culture often advocates.

The introduction of the television in the 1950s, for example, has had a profound impact on people's daily lives. Moreover, the growth of ICT has also influenced a lot of people's lives with its introduction of e-mail, chat rooms and blogging. As long as the technological facilities are available, personal communication between individuals is possible, regardless of the distance separating them. However, the world has not only become practicably smaller — new spaces, such as the internet, have simultaneously shaped a new dimension in our lives. (Castells 1997) refers to the present era as the information age. The emergence of the information super-highway and international and global media networks such as BBC-World, CNN or Al-Jazeera, as well as national and local media connected to global media networks, provide us daily with news from all over the globe (Kellner 1995). The world is increasingly becoming a global village because people's lives — irrespective of their specific location — are connected with other parts of the world through the media. The news of oppressed Afghan women in burkas does not leave us unaffected. Less than sixty years ago the average citizen may barely have known that Afghanistan existed.

At the local level, globalization has not led just to what some commentators argue to be an 'Americanization' of traditional cultures. It has also increased interpersonal international cultural exchanges via migration, tourism and exchange studentship. Many homogeneous societies have been transformed into multicultural communities in which people from different cultural backgrounds and ethnicities live together.

The development of multicultural societies has certainly not been without its problems, or its detractors. The unsettling re-emergence of extremist political parties, the segregation of cultures and even ethnic riots, illustrate the problematic side of socio-cultural integration at the local level. In a world in which financial capital and many goods can be moved freely from one country to another, the tightening of immigration laws seems to be 'deglobalizing'. Socio-cultural factors therefore not only change as a result of globalization, they can be causes, as well as challenges to the process of globalization itself.

4.3. Cross-cultural interaction

Many developments in the globalization process are causing worldwide changes in culture, but does this mean that a unified world culture is emerging? Coca-Cola's famous 1970s advertisement in which children representing cultures from around the world were singing and, of course, drinking Coke symbolized the emergence of a 'global culture'. Some commentators even speak about cultural imperialism or 'McDonaldisation' (Ritzer 1993; Ritzer 1998). This perspective is based; however, on the assumption that Western cultural elements are uncritically absorbed by non-Western nations and those cultural inflows are suppressing existing local meanings and forms (Schuerkens 2003).

A second theory refers to cultural differentiation or lasting difference. According to this view, the future will be characterized by a mosaic of immutably different cultures and civilization's (Nederveen Pieterse 2004). Huntington (Huntington 1993) argues that world politics is entering a new phase and that the fundamental source of conflict in this new world order will be cultural. The increasing interaction between peoples of different civilization's will 'intensify civilization consciousness and awareness of differences between civilizations and commonalities of civilizations'. He envisions that 'civilization identity will be increasingly important in the future' and that the world will be shaped in large measure by the interactions among seven or eight major civilization's (i.e., cultural entities), which include Western, Confucian, Japanese, Islamic,

Hindu, Slavic-Orthodox, Latin-American, and possibly African civilization. However, Huntington's views have given rise to extensive debates and his argument has been widely rejected (Nederveen Pieterse 2004). It is my personal view looking at the present climate conditions in the Global Village, The great divisions among human mankind and the dominating source of conflict will be cultural, Nation states will remain the most powerful actors in world affairs, but the principal conflicts of global politics will occur between nations and groups of different civilizations. The clash of civilization will dominate the Global village with the fault lines between civilizations and these will draw the battle lines of the future.

A third theory argues that local cultures are more robust and adaptive than the rhetoric of globalization would have us believe: a well-established viewpoint among social-cultural scientists considers globalization as a process of hybridization that gives rise to a global mélange (Nederveen Pieterse 2004). Cultural hybridization or cultural mixing refers to processes of local absorption of cultural flows and the mixture between global and local cultural elements. Inflowing cultural elements, such as television series, Western consumer articles and values introduced by migrants, can become elements of the local daily life, often in changed forms and adapted to the local context (Schuerkens 2003). (Hannertz 1996) argues, for example, that the local is the area 'where the global, or what has been local somewhere else, also has some chance of making itself at home'.

4.4. Towards an understanding of the concept of globalization

In any discussion about globalization very few of the debate's participants deny the existence of the phenomenon. Nowadays, knowledge in which cultural exchanges have been widening, has been increasingly expanding and international communication has been intensifying, the phenomenon of translation has become fundamental. It is widely accepted that we all live in a globalizing world. The debates and protests emphasize how important it is to measure globalization. Without doing so, it is impossible to assess the severity or benefits of its effects and how it should be managed — if, in fact, it can even be managed. The winners and losers from structural changes that globalization seems to accelerate are the prime political actors in the debates. In direct contrast to economic determinism, the role of the actors, or collectivities of actors within this dimension is both to shape and be influenced by the Globalizing of the capitalist economy. As mentioned previously, globalization became a prominent topic from the early 1980s.

Until that time, the topic was irregularly discussed. While deindustrialization in developed economies has long been a concern, it is moot as to why the most recent wave of globalization has been such a hot issue. Each perspective on globalization emphasizes different factors as the key elements behind the contemporary impact of this phenomenon. Moreover, they each presuppose a different definition of globalization. In our opinion, rather than attempting to define globalization and determine its effects by emphasizing particular aspects or factors, it would be far more useful to adopt a more multi-dimensional, pluralistic approach. T h i s will prevent an over-simplification of the complexities involved in understanding globalization, while permitting a flexible definition of contemporary globalization. Globalization has become far more than a social commentator's buzzword in modern times. Whether the world may have flattened or not, measuring globalization is now a central concern in academia, business, the mass and specialized media as well as in policy-making circles. Many analyses of globalization emphasize different elements of the phenomenon, often presupposing a different and idiosyncratic definition of globalization. In our opinion, rather than attempting to narrowly define globalization and determine its effects by emphasizing specific aspects, it is far more useful to adopt a more multi-dimensional, pluralistic approach that avoids an over-simplification of the complexities involved in understanding contemporary globalization. In order to be in a position to evaluate the consequences of globalization, objective indicators, such as the Maastricht Globalization Index (MGI) (Martens and Zywietz 2006), developed by the Dutch research institute ICIS, Maastricht University, and the Globalization index produced by the KOF Swiss Economic Institute (Dreher 2006) are extremely insightful.

To assess the extent to which any country is more (or less) globalized at any particular point in time requires much more than employing data on flows of trade or foreign direct investment. Both political integration and social integration are also important for a range of issues that affect social welfare. For example, in the absence of restrictions on capital mobility, a country is more likely to competitively lower taxes or offer subsidies to attract investment, the closer is a potential host country's culture to that of a source country and the easier it is to exchange information. Lower taxes may also lower the social safety net. On the other hand, political integration may ameliorate a potential 'race to the bottom', which may be induced by economic globalization. There is further belief of some scholars and their argument is that not only does the increased mobility of capital erode the tax base, reducing the state's ability to fund welfare programs, but by shifting taxes onto labor, the capacity of the state to redistribute is reduced.

The MGI and KOF index are founded on the idea that globalization includes social, political as well as economic factors (and, in case of the MGI, ecological factors as well). Specifically, globalization is defined as the intensification of cross-national economic, political, cultural, social and technological interactions that lead to the establishment of trans-national structures and the integration of economic, political and social processes on a global scale (see (Dreher, Gaston et al. 2008), (Rennen and Martens 2003)).

The question is How do we measure Globalization in the context of KOF?

The KOF index is published by Swiss federal institute of technology Zurich, and measures Globalization from social, economic and political dimension, The KOF index is presented in a scale 1 to 100, where greater number represents a more advanced Globalization. Each dimension is subdivided with factors and their percentiles add up to 100.Each factor has a variable, which also add up to 100%

In order to operationalize this definition, the KOF index further defines

- Economic globalization as the long distance flows of goods, capital and services as well as information and perceptions that accompany market exchanges;
- Political globalization by the diffusion of government policies;

- Social globalization as the spread of ideas, information, images and people.

- The social dimension is categorized into personal contact, information flows and cultural proximity.

The first two are calculated based on transfer payment, incoming and outgoing tourism, international telecom traffic, proportion of internet users, volume of foreign newspaper traded. Cultural proximity is particularly measured with level of foreign infrastructure installed in local society, such as the number of McDonald's and IKEA in a nation per capita. Last but rather important, membership of international organization is considered the most essential in the political dimension of KOF index. Globalization is also measured politically with the number of Embassies in a country, international treaties signed by a country and participation in the UN Security Council Missions.

A potential danger associated with indices of globalization is that countries in the top ten of a globalization index ranking are regarded as the most merit worthy. However, to evaluate the rankings, we need to consider what it means to be at the top, middle or bottom of a. globalization ranking. We provide such an evaluation in Measuring Globalization - Gauging its Consequences (Dreher, Gaston et al. 2008). For example, when the natural environment and the trade in conventional arms are included in these indices, like the MGI does, countries may be more globalized when their ecological footprint is high or when they are actively involved in arms trading. Not necessarily a good thing. On the other hand, most economists consider the average effect of globalization on the economy to be positive. One of the virtues of indices of globalization is that they provide a tool with which to empirically examine and discuss such widely held beliefs. However, as stressed above, other non-economic elements are equally important in the globalization debate.

4.5. Conclusion

Overall, globalization cannot be universally good or bad. Efforts to protect local culture from the homogenizing effects of globalization are often intertwined with other, sometimes questionable, motives, including economic protectionism and the political suppression of ideas. Because the topic of culture can, almost by definition, encompass almost every human endeavor, it is often difficult to draw lines around what are legitimate cultural activities, worthy of special protective measures. According to (Dreher, Gaston et al. 2008), globalization increases economic growth, but also inequality. It is beneficial to the natural environment in the medium term, but harmful in the longer run. Deunionisation increases as a consequence of globalization. How to weigh, e.g., the positive impact of globalization on economic growth against reduced deionization or increased inequality is not obvious and, clearly, the overall judgment depends on one's preferences and political inclinations.

In most economists' reading, the average effect of globalization on the economy appears to be positive in net terms. In the USA, the term Globalization often has negative connotations, for many, it represents a threat to their jobs, livelihood and way of life. Though many Americans think of it as a dirty word, "Globalization "" actually has been a catalyst for positive change as well. Here are four ways that Globalization has had a positive impact of the world economy.

1. More efficient markets

Efficient markets should be what every economy strives for, essentially, the sign of an efficient market is where there is an equilibrium between what buyers are willing to pay for a good or service and what sellers are willing to sell for a good or service.

2. Increased Competition

With more competitors to fight over market share, each country or company has to constantly look to improve their goods or services or create more value for their customers. This means better products and sometime lower prices, which is always a good sign for the buyers.

3. Stabilized Security

Although this may seem kind of twisted since there is so much violence that still goes on in the world, the fact remains that Globalization has halted many conflicts that c could have turned ugly if their country's financial health didn't depend on the other.

4. More wealth equality throughout the world

Globalization may have stopped you from buying another Flat screen TV, but it also helped countless people in developing countries put food on their table for their families. There is a silver lining to it all.

think of it However, it is obvious that globalization also produces losers. This is hardly surprising, because globalization affects the underlying structure of economies causing the shift of workers and other factors of production from industry to industry as well as from country to country. According to normative economic theory, the losers from these structural shifts should be compensated from the winners' gains. Of course, it is stating the obvious that they most often are not. This is one reason for the visible concern about globalization. Transfers from the winners to the losers of globalization are more difficult to implement in practice than in theory. First, the losers have to be identified. Second, they have to be compensated without producing adverse incentives to the economy as a whole. While there is now sufficient empirical evidence to at least tentatively conclude on the first of these issues, the second, more pressing one, remains as one of the most challenging research questions for social scientists.

5. THE DEBATE

When all the benefits and costs of globalization are taken into consideration, for some it is a process that should be supported while for others it should be avoided. In this part advocate and opponent institutions and ideas are analyzed.

5.1. Advocates of Globalization: Neo-Liberal View

"" Neo"" means we are talking about a new kind of liberalism. So, what was the old kind? The liberal school of economics became famous in Europe when Adam Smith, an Scottish Economist, published a book in 1776 called The Wealth Of Nations. He and others advocated the abolition of Government intervention in economic matters No restrictions on manufacturing, no barriers to commerce, no tariffs, he said free trade was the best way for a nation's economy to develop.

Such ideas were "" liberal"" in the sense of no controls. This application of individualism encouraged "" Free Enterprise "" "Free Competition "'____ which came to mean, free for the capitalists to make huge profits as they wished.

Established in Sweden as a non-profit organization World Economic Forum (WEF) is independent and international which was first designed by a group of businessmen in January 1971 with the leadership of European Commission and European Industrial Associations. It was founded as European Management Forum in Geneva, Sweden. However, the collapse of Bretton Woods fixed exchange rate system in 1973 and the Arab-Israel enlarged the focus of these meetings from management to economic and social issues and political leaders were invited to Davos in January 1974. European Management Forum changed its name as World Economic Forum in 1987 and tried to enlarge its vision in order to solve international conflicts.

Organization endeavors for a worldwide governance system which is based on not only the rules but also on values. Its motto is "entrepreneurship in the global public interest". Its members (1000 largest firms that have global activities, rank among top companies within their industry and/or country and have a leading role in shaping the future of their industry and/or region and 200 relatively small firms from developing countries) believe that without economic development, social development is infeasible and vice versa.

The organization's vision has 3 dimensions. These are:

- To be the most important organization that forms and strengthen leader global communities,
- To be the creative force that shape global, regional and industrial strategies,
- To be a catalyst in the choices of communities which have global attempts for the development of the world.

Members get advantage as they recognize and affect two new developments:

- The key problems of the world cannot be solved by governments, business or civil society alone and
- Strategic foresights in a world characterized as complex, fragile and synchronized cannot

be achieved passively. These foresights can be achieved through continuous interaction with partners and those who are best informed in their fields of study.

• Therefore in order to realize its mission the WEF formed an integrated value chain through the inclusion of world leaders into the communities, inspiring them with strategic foresights and evoking them with initiatives.

Another globalization advocate is the Washington Consensus which was initiated in 1989 by John Williamson in order to support the countries that had experienced crisis through Washington D.C. based institutions such as the IMF, the World Bank (WB) and the US Department of Treasury and that comprises of ten special economic policy recommendations (fiscal policy discipline, redistribution of public expenditures, tax reform, marked-determined interest rate, competitive exchange rate, trade liberalization, FDI inflow liberalization, privatization, elimination of restrictive terms and the protection of property rights) that are taught to be a "standard" reform package.

Since its initiation, the concept "Washington Consensus" The Washington Consensus is a set of 10 economic policy prescription considered to constitute the "STANDARD" reform package promoted for crisis-wracked developing countries by Washington, DC- Based institutions such as the International Monetary Fund (IMF) World Bank, and the US Treasury Department. has attained a second meaning that is sometimes called neo-liberalism or market fundamentalism where markets have bigger roles while governments have limited roles.

Especially with this second and broader formulation Washington Consensus has been the target of individuals and groups' tough criticisms seeing it as the way to open less developed countries to MNCs and the investments of their owners in the first world economies.

These criticisms often refer to 1999-2002 Argentina economic crises where they think the policies of Washington Consensus are defective because Argentina applied most of the policies recommended by the Consensus.

Many trade liberalization critics like Noam Chomsky, Susan George and Naomi Klein denote the Washington Consensus as the gate of exploitation of the labor markets of under-developed countries by the firms of developed countries. The decreases in the tariffs and trade restrictions let the free movement of goods according to market among countries, but because of tight visa applications labor does not move freely. This creates an economic climate that goods are produced in under developed countries with low labor cost and then exported to prosperous first world economies with high mark-ups taken by MNCs. Criticisms claim that the workers in the third world economies are poor; although they take higher wages than the ones before trade liberalization, these wages are melting with inflation. While the owners of MNCs get richer, the workers in the first world economies become unemployed.

Some criticisms or all of them are denied by the advocates of Washington Consensus as a result of some realizations. For example the inflation rates are at its lowest level in recent years. Workers of the factories established by foreign capital earn more and have better working conditions than those working in domestic firms. In most countries of Latin America the economic growth is at its highest levels and the debt services are at its lowest level relative to the economy. Despite these macroeconomic developments, poverty and inequality are high in Latin America. The world Bank released in September last year the per capita income in Latin America, Argentina reports the highest per capita income of $7,600 followed by Uruguay with $5,900, Chile captures the sub Continent's third spot with $4,740 followed by Brazil with $4,420. Mexico ranks fifth with $4,400. Again one third of the population lacks electricity and sanitation and presumably 10 million children suffer from malnutrition.

5.2. Opponents of Globalization:
Anti-Globalist Movement

The antiglobalization movement is pluralistic and to a certain extent contradictory. Groups that have been involved include traditional and autonomous labor unions, art groups, landless peasants groups, indigenous groups, socialists, communists, anarchists, autonomous groups. Trotskyist, parts of ecology movement and the feminist movement. Third world initiatives Civil rights groups, students, religious groups, human rights groups, groups from the unemployment movement, traditional left-wing parties, critical intellectuals, and so forth from all over the world. This network is characterized as a global network of networks, a a movement of social movement, a universal protest movement and a coalition of coalitions. It aims at reclaiming the common character of goods and services that are increasingly privatized by agreements such as General Agreement on Trade in Services (GATS) and the Agreement of Trade Related Aspects of intellectual Property Rights (TRIPS)

In one of his speech at the University of Houston the Nobel Prize winner Rigoberta Manchu said "Globalization —the intensification of capital and particularly communication systems- affect the life of not only the indigenous but also the poor people. When one talks about free trade, he/she does not talk about small and medium sized commercial sectors but rather huge monopolies.

Anti-globalists focus not on the figures like GDP that are announced by the WB and its derivatives but on the indices like Happy Planet Index. The Happy

Planet Index (HP) is an index of human well-being and environmental impact that was introduce by the new Economics Foundation (NEF) in July 2006. The index is weighted to give progressively higher scores to nations with lower ecological footprints. calculated by New Economics Foundation. This index focuses on interrelated vital consequences like social resolution, death of democracy, fast and extensive deterioration of environment, spread of new diseases, increasing poverty and alienation.

The organization that is at the position of the representative of anti-globalist movement is the World Social Forum (WSF). The World Social Forum is an annual meeting of civil society organization, first held in Brazil, which offers a self-conscious effort to develop an alternative future through the championing of counter-hegemonic globalization.

WSF is a meeting arranged by the members of anti-globalization or alter-globalization movement annually to coordinate world campaigns, share and refine organizing strategies, and to inform each other about movements around the world and their issues. Its motto is "Another world is possible". It tends to meet in January when its "great capitalist rival", the WEF is meeting in Davos, Switzerland.

WSF has encouraged the organizing of many regional social forums, i.e. European, Asian and Mediterranean Social Forums, and many local and national social forums such as Turkish, Liverpool and Boston Social Forums.

The World Social Forum is an open meeting space for reflective thinking, democratic debates of ideas, formulation of proposals, free exchange of experience and interlinking for effective action, by groups and movements of civil society that are opposed to neoliberalism and to domination of the world by capital and any form of imperialism, and are committed to building a planetary society directed towards fruitful relationship among Human mankind and between it and the earth.

WSF defines itself and its mission in its charter of principles. According to the charter the Forum is and open platform to everyone who contributes to the exchange of ideas, proposals, experiences and inter-linkages for effective action in a democratic environment. It is universal. It refuses the process of globalization that serves the interests of MNCs. It aims to unite world non-governmental organizations but it is not a representative of such organizations. No one is authorized with the representation of the Forum. The organizations that attend Forum meetings can freely declare their ideas. The Forum has a plural structure and open to differences provided that they respect the principles of the Forum; it is an organization that does not have religious, statist, military or biased dimensions.

The Forum contradicts all repressive economies, views of development and history and the usage of these as a repression factor by governments. It also contradicts the racist, sexist and environment pollutant effects of capitalist globalization. It encourages national and international linkages among organizations and social movements in order to ease the achievement of its goals. It allows local to global movements by its participants.

Besides WSF, there are other anti-globalist organizations. Their globalization oppositions vary in terms of scale and content. The major of these movements are:

International Forum on Globalization (IFG): Founded January 1994 in san Francisco, with two goals (1) Expose the multiple effects of economic Globalization in order to stimulate debate, and (2) Seek to reverse the globalization process by encouraging ideas and activities which revitalize Local economies and communities, and ensure long term ecological stability.

It is an establishment constituted by activists, economists, scholars and researchers that analyses and criticizes the cultural, social, politic and environmental effects of economic globalization and runs north-south research and is instructive. The most important criticism of the organization is the lack of criticism for "free trade" and "neo-liberalism" or the institutions and treaties such as World Trade Organization (WTO), IMF and North Atlantic Free Trade Agreement (NAFTA). IFG encourages more equal, democratic and ecologic economies that can be alternative to neo-liberalism or to globalization. In its alternative search, the Forum highlights living democracy, supporting local, ecologic sustainability, joint heritage, diversity, human rights, business and life, food security, equity and precaution principle. Besides, the Forum claims that the institutions of globalization, IMF, WTO and WB are under legitimacy crisis.

People's Global Action (PGA): From the 23rd to the 26th of February of 1998, grassroots movements of all continents met in Geneva to Launch a worldwide coordination network of resistance to the Global market, a new alliance of struggle and solidarity and called Peoples" Global Action against "Free "trade and the WTO (PGA). That was the birth of this Global Tool for communication and coordination for all those who fight the destruction of humanity and the planet of capitalism and build local alternatives to Globalization. In this framework, the movement has a more radical attitude than other organizations.

Corpwatch (CW): The organization was first established in 1996 under the name of Transnational Resource & Action Center (TRAC) and then in March 2001 took the name, CorpWatch. The organization drew attention with the analyses of poor working conditions of Nike in Vietnam and Enron before its crash, and firms that make profit from wars. Organization defines itself as globalization opponent in the subjects of human rights, social justice, environmental sustainability, peace, negative economic realizations, corporate transparency and accountability.

Friends of the Earth (FE): The organization which was established in 1971 mostly deals with environmental problems. Organization has some targets about climate change, recycling, energy-saving houses, organic agriculture and the protection of nature. It is one of the 70 national groups around the world which make up the friends of the Earth network of environmental organization. It is usually referred to just Friends of the Earth within its home coutries.Organization runs with the ideas of "there is tomorrow", "everyone gets a fair share" and "change the rules for a better economy". In this framework, the organization opposes enterprises and globalization in case they affect environment negatively.

Different cultures have been brought into closer contact with each other. Multiculturalism is an aspect of globalization. Harvey sees this situation as chaotic and disorientating. People are moving around the world, sharing cultures so that our ideas of race and nationality are changing. He fears that we are losing our identity. Others think it enriches us and allows marginalized voices to be heard.

What implications does this have for architecture and design? The critic Frédéric Migayrou concluded that: "Architects are coming to the fore within a new international coherence that is thoroughly transcultural and hybrid." There are two basic responses. On one hand there has been a spread of uniform, homogeneous architecture around the world that stamps out local culture. On the other hand, there is a reaction against this. Some architects are trying to resist globalization and emphasize local character.

A major factor is the rise of global corporations and financial institutions that dominate the world economy. These are some of the most powerful institutions in the world. For example, the headquarters of the Honk Kong and Shanghai Banking Corporation in Hong Kong was designed by Norman Foster, a British architect. The fact that a British architect was commissioned by an Asian corporation is itself an example of cross-cultural exchange. It has a steel exoskeleton that supports the structure – it celebrates technology and engineering by exposing all the functional and structural elements. The components of the building were manufactured all over the world — the structural steel came from Britain; the aluminum cladding came from the USA.

The HSBC tower was the most expensive building ever built at the time. It's built on a megalomaniacal scale that asserts the power of the HSBC Corporation. The structural form is deliberately muscular and macho. HSBC calls itself the world's local bank, which is a very friendly, disingenuous way of saying that it dominates the global market. The bank was founded in 1865 by Thomas Sutherland, a Scot, to finance British trade in the Far East. Therefore, a global corporation like this actually began as a remnant of the British Empire. Globalization can be seen as a new form of imperialism. The HSBC logo is derived from the Hong Kong and Shanghai Banking Corporation's 19th century house flag, which itself is based on the Scottish flag, with the diagonal cross.

Some people see globalization primarily as an economic phenomenon. National economies all over the world are becoming linked together because of international trade. Countries are becoming more and more dependent on each other. Globalization is undeniably a capitalist process. The fall of the Berlin Wall and the collapse of the Soviet Union symbolized the failure of Communist and the victory of capitalism. Left wing critics of globalization define it as a global economic system dominated by international institutions that are more powerful than any individual national government, so they cannot be controlled by democratic processes. But it is more than just economics. There has been a huge increase in social and cultural exchange across national borders.

5.3. Common challenges for the global enterprise

Global enterprises face many challenges. Some of those challenges are identical with those found in domestic or international arenas. For example, a common challenge for all businesses is to earn a profit; for a voluntary organization the common challenge is to meet social objectives. In an international country-to-country era, businesses face currency conversion challenges that also persist in a global world. Finally, competition is a reality for all businesses wherever they operate. In addition, global businesses face challenges that emerge from a more global world. It is important to recognize that while every organization faces these challenges, the exact nature of the challenge and organizational responses to them will vary, and this is something that is demonstrated in the following sections.

5.4.1. Challenge 1: Problems that Cannot be Solved but Must be Managed

A paradox is a statement or proposition that, despite apparently sound reasoning from true premises, leads to a self-contradictory or a logically unacceptable conclusion. A Paradox involves contradictory yet interrelated elements that exist simultaneously and persist over time. seems contradictory. Writing in The Age of Paradox, Charles Handy (1994) identified nine paradoxical challenges or situations that cannot be resolved so much as managed. At the global level, one paradox is how all nations can benefit economically from competitive business activities since competition usually implies that there will be winners and losers. At the level of national governments, paradox includes balancing between global interests and domestic interests. At the organizational level, paradoxes might include cooperating to compete, and managers might see profitability as a trade-off between self-interest and the interests of a larger society. At the individual level, the statement expresses an apparent paradox: "the more I do, the less I get done." Students often face this paradox: "the more I learn, the more questions I have." Individuals also face a paradox when they are encouraged to think in linear and process-oriented fashions; to be autonomous and yet to be team members; to have a full life and yet to devote all free time to the organization.

A Center for Creative Leadership Conference created a list of these and similar organizational paradoxes or trade-offs such as balancing individual achievement against team achievement, focusing on people or on the bottom line, emphasis on processes or on results, and viewing organizations as engines for economic development or for human development (Tornow, 1994). In personal lives and professional worlds, many are taught to look at paradoxes and other challenges as problems that need solving. However, according to Charles Handy, a major managerial challenge of paradox is to learn to live with it. In effect, managing paradox is the first global challenge all organizations face: there are problems that cannot be solved so much as managed. Few certainties characterize globalization, but one among them is the increased number of multiple and competing objectives every person and organization faces. In view of cultural, political, economic, and other differences throughout the world, it is currently impossible to reconcile many of these objectives. Thus, one of the primary challenges associated with globalization is balancing conflicting and/or competing objectives such as the apparent trade-off between profits and social responsibility, individual and collective interests, autonomy and collaboration, innovation and order, heterogeneity and homogeneity.

5.4.2. Sample Problems that Cannot be Solved so much as Managed

Global pharmaceutical firms invest in research and development that cannot be recaptured in many developing economies. Yet, growing networks for medical information make it impossible to withhold knowledge about useful remedies; often the formulas are copied with no reimbursement to the originator, and few worldwide legal conventions provide universal protection. Merck's product Crixivan has been shown effective against the AIDs disease, but neither Merck nor its subcontractors can produce sufficient supplies worldwide to keep up with the spread of this disease. Many companies face challenges that cannot be solved when markets and economies take a turn for the worse. Grupo Televisa suffered financial difficulties with the breakdown of the peso and losses due to foreign investment. Although these were problems that Televisa could not solve themselves NAFTA helped by eliminating trade barriers. Companies are encouraged to grow, but face risks when doing so. This causes a decline in the profitability that investors seek. Not so with a complex problem situation. There is no definitive solution. Infect, we are not even sure exactly how to describe the problem condition. To make matters worse, different stakeholders may have entirely different interpretations, not to mention different ultimate agendas and conflicting expectations. For example, when the market was growing rapidly Matsushita Electric intended to grow via US expansion with a new semiconductor plant. But Matsushita encountered delays, the market slowed, and the semiconductor plan was abandoned. The company is believed to have lost around $90 million instead of fostering growth.

Balancing the risks of growth is a problem that cannot be solved so much as managed.

Mercy Corps faces risks when it decides how to use limited resources. It must choose the right project to provide the greatest long-term social benefits. Choosing the wrong project reduces their ability to leverage resources worldwide. As Sony expands throughout the world and becomes an ever-larger company, its organizational structure becomes very large and complicated. Sony has recognized this and formulated new corporate strategies to deal with the problem, but still must manage the trade-off between being small enough to be innovative and large enough to manage all their operations worldwide. During times of economic slowdown companies face challenges in trying to maintain a balance between lay-offs and social responsibility. After eliminating jobs in Germany, Siemens drew criticism from the union. They were accused of being short sighted as well as adhering to a hire-and-fire policy. The union argues that Siemens cannot just fire employees during an economic slump, then rehire when times are better. At the same time, investors expect Siemens to be profitable, and this may be hard to achieve if they have too many workers on their payrolls.

The World Health Organization is faced with the challenge of reduced funding by the member states. This has led them to partner with large pharmaceutical companies that in turn could influence their decisions on important health issues. For example, the WHO launched a campaign against smoking, but this could benefit drug-company partners that produce nicotine replacement drugs. Balancing how to reinvent themselves as an organization concerned about lung cancer in addition to clean water or disfiguring diseases is a major challenge for WHO. In response to consumer activists who target companies regarding wages and working conditions, Mattel generated Global Manufacturing Principles. The code, called The Global Manufacturing Principal (GMP),confronts the general criticism Leveled against Voluntary codes of conduct by (a) creating detailed standards of compliance,(b) independent external monitoring of the company's compliance with its code of conduct, and (c) making full, and uncensored public disclosure of the audit findings and company's response in terms of remedial actions. principles govern Mattel factories and vendors worldwide and provide a way to manage regulations that are both beneficial to the workers and the company. But this forces Mattel to be involved not only in their own activities but also those of suppliers. Because of the large, global nature of the World Wildlife Fund, as well as the large amount of money flowing through it, the organization has had to find ways to manage corruption risk. The WWF has attempted to form alliances to assist in problem solving and to assist in avoiding corruption problems by basically implementing a check-and-balance system among countries and governments that they align with.

5.4.3. Challenge 2: Organizational Success Increasingly is Derived from Intangibles that Organizations Cannot Own

In the industrial economy, location was important to companies because it gave them control over the means of production. This was the case with the company which was situated at a location which provided road, rail and sea transportation; access to the resources of the local coal mining industry; and a skilled and plentiful workforce.

In the Global economy, however power comes not from location per se but rather from the ability to command intangible assets that make customers loyal. These assets have been identified as, competence, concepts and connections.

Rapid growth in knowledge-based industries has drawn attention to the roles intellect and knowledge play in organizations. Knowledge is critical to organizational achievement, and the ability to link and leverage knowledge is increasingly a factor for differentiating among organizations that survive (Bartlett and Ghoshal, 1989). Unlike other productive factors like land, capital, and equipment, intelligence does not belong to the organization. Further, information is not a scarce resource (Henderson, 1996), and it cannot be taken, redistributed, owned, accurately measured, or monopolized (Handy, 1994). Finally, although organizations depend heavily on knowledge as a critical resource, many do not know how to value it. Thus, many organizational resources may not be reflected in public valuations of the enterprise. The "bricks and mortar" upon which traditional valuations are built often do not capture the value of "clicks" established through Internet knowledge and information transfer. Knowledge frequently is leveraged via means of intangible processes such as relationship building, or trust enhancement. Intangibles based on qualities like these are difficult to measure, assess, or implement. Rosabeth Kanter (1995: 152) believes these knowledge-based intangible assets are of three kinds:

Put simply, the concept, competence and connections relate to the roles that intellect and knowledge now play in organizations. It is the ability to link knowledge in creative ways that is essential factor. When asked to identify the critical skills that were needed in today's company, the manager was quite clear that knowledge is everything. If we know the price is going to be "X"

We can be successful. Communication and market knowledge are the vital skills.

Unlike important productive factors such as land, capital and equipment that contributed to early industrialization, intelligence does not belong to the organization; it cannot be taken, redistributed,owned, accurately measured, or monopolized. The company in common with other organizations cannot redistribute intelligence nor can they prevent others from acquiring it, and they cannot preserve it. Companies must attend not only to their current competition but also to their" invisible "enemies-unfamiliar companies outside the industry possessing a technological capability that could be a threat if transferred to new markets.

The intangible quality of knowledge is reflected in relationships and also in employee skills and abilities. A change in the employee base, particularly among top management, often results in a knowledge deficit or increase, and many analysts examine these changes to anticipate the likely effect on an organization.

54.4. Examples of Increased Reliance on Intangibles

Despite widespread acceptance that intangible assets such as brands are critical to the prospects of a business, they have traditionally been put in the too-difficult box-in terms of both their ongoing management and communicating their value. The fact that it can be difficult to obtain the information needed to manage and enhance the value of brands or patents, together with the sensitivity of that information, has held many companies back.

Philips lost market share when compact-disc technology was used by other companies and in other countries even though a patent was in place. The Boeing Company is committed to developing the human capital of their employees. The Boeing Company annually commits a minimum of $4.5 million towards education, training, and career-development training. For Sony it is very important to hire, retain, and foster knowledge workers. Furthermore, Sony offers a pleasant working environment where people can make the most of their abilities. Panasonic's founder was famous for promoting the concept of coexistence and coprosperity in countries in which Panasonic conducts business. The core values of IKEA were codified in Ingvar Kamprad's 1976 "Furniture Dealer's Testament" which are taught to all IKEA employees. Shiseido depends on connections with prominent and talented artists, designers, and places to support its business activity. For example, Shiseido appointed a French artist, Serge Lutens, as its international image creator. Because of the increasing importance and complex nature of environmental problems, the World Wildlife Federation increasingly relies on its employees and volunteers to use current technology and practices to solve environmental problems. Mercy Corps subscribes to the idea that "few firms could achieve industry leadership or be competitive globally without some global strategic partners." One of Mercy Corps' strengths is its ability to partner with a multitude of corporations, government agencies, foundations, faith organizations, the United Nations, and the World Bank. However, the resulting synergies are often intangible.

5.4.5. Challenge 3: Organizations Increasingly Manage Many Forms of Diversity

Managing Diversity

While diversity provides many benefits to the organisation, it's also essential for managers and employees to understand how to manage diversity to the organisation's as well as their own benefit.

Organisations and managers alike need to consciously take steps and initiatives to encourage more heterogeneous groups that ultimately lead to better market understanding and decision making.

This requires managers to understand their own backgrounds and behaviours better and understand how it affects their perspectives and decision making.

A successful manager should be able to manage diversity by building a culture of tolerance through education, training, communication and conflict management strategies.

The world's increasing globalization requires more interaction among people from diverse backgrounds. People no longer live and work in an insular environment, they are now part of worldwide economy competing within a global framework. For this reason, profit or non-profit organizations need to become more diversified to remain competitive. Maximizing and capitalizing on workplace diversity is a prominent issue for management.

Diversity of people— their color, their nationality, their gender— emerged as an issue almost simultaneously around the globe, fostered by global economics and immigration, government regulations, and transnational human-rights mandates. Whatever the motivation, many in organizations initially viewed increased diversity as a problem. Initial business responses to the "problem" of diversity often followed national legislation based on differences of color, gender, or nationality. Many firms assumed that assimilation was the most desirable response to diversity. In other words, early business efforts involved training women, ethnic minorities, and/or immigrants to behave more like existing employees. Organizational managers soon discovered the impracticalities of assimilation, recognizing that diversity of experience is exactly what is required in a more diverse and global world. The boundaries of diversity also have expanded. Studies of diversity show that sometimes similarities are found where differences had been assumed. Organizations also house not only diverse people, but diverse systems, diverse structures, diverse ways of thinking and acting, and diverse processes. All are aspects of managing diversity.

5.4.6. Examples of Managing Diversity

A manager needs to be able to understand the cultural nuances before providing feedback to employees from different countries and backgrounds.

Another important way to ensure diversity inclusion is to make the workplace and policies more compatible for inclusion of the diversity.

For example: Providing flexi-hours to employees, allowing employees to choose their own holidays according to their religious preferences.

Providing a workplace that is conducive to accommodate the needs of employees with physical disabilities is also very important.

Diversity Awareness

Diversity awareness deals with creating a workplace where individuals understand and respect the differences in race, gender, religion, cultural values and thinking styles.

A huge element of this understanding is self-awareness which plays a significant role in helping employees understand their own cultural biases, prejudices and stereotypes.

To create diversity awareness, it's essential to improve self-awareness of the managers through assessment tools and training.

Mattel increased diversity in its product range to stabilize sales. This was done by implementing a mixture of year-round toys with seasonal toys. As a result of re-engineering efforts to improve market share, Philips Components initiated a joint venture with LG Electronics of South Korea. Philips expects further growth through alliances and acquisitions. One reason for these alliances is that it has become necessary to locate facilities in many places to attract talent. Thus, this example shows that diversity in structure and with people often are managed simultaneously. IKEA moves into markets slowly, and looks at how they can complement existing trends in a market. This "fusion" helps to minimize culture clash with employees and customers. IKEA job applications in all countries have the following statement at the top, setting the tone for celebrating diversity from an employee's first interaction with the company: "In our IKEA family we want to keep the human being in the center and to support each other' —Ingvar Kamprad." Honda

Motor Company believes that cultural differences can be a source of extraordinary performance results when integration of different perspectives results in a unique competitive advantage. The paradox is that diversity can mean difficulties, but diversity is also the cornerstone for creativity. The philosophy of Honda is that diversity begins with respect for the individual.

Based on this philosophy, thousands of diverse individuals work together as a team toward a common goal. Honda implements dozens of internal training programs to help those working in diverse groups. Unilever acknowledges the potential problems that result from cultural diversity, but the company believes it gains an advantage by honoring differences between people as well as similarities. Unilever has implemented many corporate diversity initiatives dealing with communication and training that enhances the advantages of diversity. To address diversity issues the Boeing Company's human resources department has created an internal company website devoted to diversity. The website includes information related to diversity issues such as: how employees can respect each other's differences, working with people from different cultural backgrounds, and information on diversity classes for employees and managers.

An example of how Nokia manages employee diversity is that most of the daily work is carried out by cross-functional teams within the Finnish corporate office. By drawing teams comprised from different groups, Nokia is better able to foster efficiency and productivity. For example, an accountant may be able to offer a unique perspective when confronted with a marketing problem. This cross-functionality allows employees to understand and visualize problems that Nokia faces on a company-wide scale, instead of just how it relates to them within their own department or function. Today, a company's growth and development are intrinsically linked to how that company can attract people to its organization and motivate them to create value. In April 1998, Toyota established a Corporate Diversity Department to guide the company in making diversity an integral part of every aspect of their business. Specifically, it provides strategic guidance, support for diversity initiatives, and helps develop and promote education and diversity awareness throughout the organization.

Diversity at the World Wildlife Fund goes beyond the traditional anti-discrimination, equal employment paradigm. The WWF has created an organizational structure that allows the national branches to be in control of their employment practices. This allows each national organization to hire individuals from their own country. Eastman Kodak is firmly committed to building and managing a truly diverse work force, both from a worldwide perspective and in all of its local operations. Grounded in the five Kodak values (respect, integrity, trust, credibility, and continuous improvement of personal renewal), Kodak's efforts are guided by its Global Performance Expectation on Diversity, one of six corporate business imperatives articulated by CEO George Fisher.

5.4.7. Challenge 4: Business Managers and Organizations Assume New Roles for which the Past has Not Prepared Them

All businesses produce and rely on large volumes of information - financial records, interactions with customers and other business contacts, employee details, regulatory requirements and so on. It's too much to keep track of - let alone use effectively - without the right systems.

Responsibilities and tasks can be delegated as your business grows, but without solid management information systems you cannot manage effectively. The larger your business grows, the harder it is to ensure that information is shared and divergent functions work together effectively. Putting the right infrastructure in place is an essential part of helping your business to grow.

Business research necessarily looks at the past and the present more than at the future. However, global firms face a future that could be quite different from the past. For example, most worldwide business research studies manufacturing firms, but today services such as banking, telecommunications, tourism, and education are important contributors to globalization. Service globalization may require different strategic capabilities than those used in manufacturing (Campbell and Verbeke, 1994). In practice, many assumptions about how businesses can or should operate are being re-evaluated. For example, having instituted "open book" management by making financial details available to all employees, Sara Lee managers realized a first step was to teach employees how to interpret financial data. Thereafter, managers observed employees were just as adept as they in recognizing gains and losses, and perhaps more adept in finding ways to balance them (Lee, 1994). This sudden empowerment among employees meant that managers had to share roles that previously were theirs alone. The examples below illustrate other events for which managers were ill prepared.

5.4.8. Examples of Challenges for which Managers are Not Prepared

During a recent training session, Tony Tomanek, ERC Senior Consultant, Training & Organizational Development, saw first-hand what can happen when a breakdown in communication occurs between employees and their supervisors.

"I had a woman come up to me during a break in the training session," Tomanek said. "She was very emotional and teary eyed. In her seven years with the company, not once had her boss asked how her weekend was. Her boss was a driver, with a direct,

'Don't waste my time, I don't want to know about your personal life' kind of attitude.

"At a superficial level, that seems OK," Tomanek continued. "But employees sometimes feel they need interpersonal communication to achieve a certain level of trust. If an employee feels that their supervisor doesn't care about them, they can become disengaged and even tune the boss out."

Maintaining good lines of communication is just one challenge managers and supervisors face. The management of conflict and performance, and management of potential liabilities can be tough hurdles to clear, too.

Failing to address any of these issues can lead to damaging consequences for an organization. Companies, though, can be proactive in avoiding these pitfalls through the support and development of their managers.

Here are 5 familiar challenges for managers and supervisors - and some practical ways to deal with them.

Communicate.

Managers frequently are not aware of the quality of their communication or, as Tomanek's example illustrates, how their communication or interpersonal style are perceived by their employees.

You can help managers understand their unique communication and interpersonal style and how to "flex" this style in different situations by providing communication templates, scripts, tips or checklists. Engage in role-play or dialogue with the manager to help them practice their skills and identify opportunities for improvement. Additionally, educate managers on common communication breakdowns and how to avoid them and encourage managers to notice signs of communication problems (misunderstandings, consistent performance problems, etc.).

When all else fails, provide a personal coach if communication problems persist

Resolve conflict.

Many managers ignore problems and do not directly address conflicts with their employees or work team.

Whether these are performance problems, conflicts among team members, issues of trust or personality clashes, managers are challenged to confront and address problems head-on and as they emerge, diffuse employees' feelings and emotions about the problem, listen to both parties' needs and desires, derive win-win solutions that lead to more productive and positive work relations, and prevent conflict in the future by nurturing positive coworker relationships and recognizing potential for conflict or problems early.

Manage performance.

Managers must balance meeting goals, managing workloads and motivating employees. These issues, coupled with the fact that many managers are ill-equipped to provide regular and constructive feedback and may not understand the importance of documenting performance, can make managing performance challenging.

To support them, build on-going performance feedback into the performance management process to ensure accountability. Create an easy method for managers to document performance like a database, log, or diary. Provide support tools for managers such as rewards, recognition, training and development to recognize and build performance. Most importantly, train managers in topics such as performance management, coaching and feedback since many will have had no experience with these.

Handle protected employees.

Most managers are not well-versed in administering ADA, FMLA and other laws that protect certain groups of employees, but unknowingly find themselves managing an employee who requires an accommodation, leave of absence or falls into a protected class.

These situations need to be handled delicately due to their legal nature, so make managers aware of:

- Legal basics such as conditions or disabilities that are protected
- How to determine essential functions and reasonable accommodations
- Requirements associated with FMLA (eligibility, length of time, etc.)

- Types of employees that are protected under law (gender, race, national origin, etc.)
- Hiring and interviewing liabilities (questions to ask/not ask, etc.)

Administer policies fairly and consistently.

One of the most familiar challenges for managers is treating employees fairly and consistently. A manager may allow policies and rules to be disregarded by some employees and not others – or may disregard employment policies altogether. "Stretching" the rules for some employees can open a range of potential liabilities and perceptions of bias and favoritism that have negative far-reaching effects in the workplace.

Be sure to write clear policies and let managers know when changes have been made. Set clear criteria for making employment decisions, particularly where managers need to distinguish between employees (recognition, reward, development, etc.). Also, clearly differentiate between the policies in which managers have discretion to implement and those in which they do not

Employee roles change when organizational purpose changes. Japanese employers less frequently endorse lifetime employment, and this means Japanese students at Tokyo University are no longer guaranteed jobs. The result is that young people in Japan increasingly look for work among smaller firms, but they were unprepared for this change. Worldwide, many larger firms are finding their newer competitors to be the women, minorities, or immigrants they themselves wouldn't hire or didn't promote. Fastest growth among small businesses in the US, Western Europe, and Japan are those established by women. Managers in many firms must learn how to work with people "not like us."

This look at characteristics of and challenges for global enterprises shows that achieving global "fit" depends on more than good intentions. Managers must juggle among multiple and sometimes competing interests put forward by forces both internal and external to the firm. The integration that connects an organization to its external environment clearly involves complex tasks. Further, it should also be clear that managers and other employees increasingly make decisions and engage in global activities that carry risks and often have a high cost of failure.

6. THE NEGATIVE EFFECT ON DEVELOPED COUNTRIES

Here will discuss the benefits and drawbacks from the point of view that globalization made in the developing countries. globalization began in a primitive form when humans first settled into different areas of the world; however, it has shown a rather steady and rapid progress in recent times and has become an international dynamic which, due to technological advancements, has increased in speed and scale, so that countries in all five continents have been affected and engaged. There are three important fields such as economic and trade processes, education and health systems and culture effects. consisting of four paragraphs. In paragraph one, the benefits and detriment of globalization in the economic and trade processes field will be discussed.

Then, in paragraph two, the impact of globalization on education and health systems in both sides will be shown. In the paragraph three, the positives and negatives of globalization on culture will be illustrated. Finally, paragraph four, will deal with conclusion and offer an opinion.

Introduction

Globalization is a process of global economic, political and cultural integration. It has made the world become a small village; the borders have been broken down between countries. "The history of globalization goes back to the second half of the twentieth century, the development of transport and communication technology led to situation where national borders appeared to be too limiting for economic activity" (Economic Globalization in Developing Countries, 2002). Globalization is playing an increasingly key role in the developing countries., globalization has certain advantages such as economic processes, technological developments, political influences, health systems, social and natural environment factors. It has a lot of benefit on our daily life. Globalization has created some new opportunities for developing countries. Such as, technology transfer holds out promise, greater opportunities to access developed countries markets, growth and improved productivity and living standards. Industrialized or developed nations are specific countries with a prominent level of economic development and meet certain socioeconomic criteria based on economic theory, such as gross domestic product (GDP), industrialization and human development index (HDI) as defined by the International Monetary Fund (IMF), the United Nations (UN) and the World Trade Organization (WTO). Using these definitions, some industrialized countries in 2016 are: United Kingdom, Belgium, Denmark, Finland, France, Germany, Japan, Luxembourg, Norway, Sweden, Switzerland and the United States.

However, it is not true that all effects of this phenomenon are positive. Because, globalization has also brought up new challenges such as, environmental deteriorations, instability in commercial and financial markets, increase inequity across and within nations. This paper evaluates the positive and negative impact of globalization on developing nations in the following proportions;

1. Economic and Trade Processes Field
2. Education and Health Systems
3. Culture Effects

1- Economic and Trade Processes Field

Globalization helps developing countries to deal with rest of the world increase their economic growth, solving the poverty problems in their country. In the past, developing countries were not able to tap on the world economy due to trade barriers. They cannot share the same economic growth that developed countries had. However, with globalization the World Bank and International Management encourage developing countries to go through market reforms and radical changes through large loans. Many developing nations began to take steps to open their markets by removing tariffs and free up their economies. The developed countries were able to invest in the developing nations, creating job opportunities for the poor people. For example, rapid growth in India and China has caused world poverty to decrease (blogspot. com.2009). It is clear to see that globalization has made the relationships between developed countries and developing nations stronger, it made each country depend on another country. According to Thirlwall (2003:13) " Developing countries depend on developed countries for resource flows and technology, but developed countries depend heavily on developing countries for raw materials, food and oil, and as markets for industrial goods". One the most important advantages of globalization are goods and people are transported easier and faster as a result free trade between countries has increased, and it decreased the possibility of war between countries. Furthermore, the growth in the communication between the individuals and companies in the world helped to raise free trade between countries and this led to growth economy. However, globalization has many economy and trade advantages in the developing countries, we must also note the many disadvantages that globalization has created for the poor countries. One reason globalization increases the inequality between the rich and poor, the benefits globalization is not universal; the richer are getting rich and the poor are becoming poorer. Many developing countries do benefit from globalization but then again, many of such nations do lag behind." In the past two decades, China and India have grown faster than the already rich nations.

However, countries like Africa still have the highest poverty rates, in fact, the rural areas of China which do not tap on global markets also suffer greatly from such prevalent poverty (blogspot.com.2009). On the other hand, developed countries set up their companies and industries to the developing nations to take advantages of low wages and this causing pollution in countries with poor regulation of pollution. Furthermore, setting up companies and factories in the developing nations by developed countries affect badly to the economy of the developed countries and increase unemployment. These studies examined the effects of several components of globalization on growth using time series cross sectional data on trade, FDI and portfolio investment. Although they provide an analysis of individual components of globalization on economic growth, some of the results are inconclusive or even contradictory. However, overall, the findings of those studies seem to be supportive of the economists' positive position, instead of the one held by the public and non-economist view

2- Education and Health Systems

Globalization contributed to develop the health and education systems in the developing countries. We can clearly see that education has increased in recent years, because globalization has a catalyst to the jobs that require higher skills set. This demand allowed people to gain higher education. Health and education are basic objectives to improve any nations, and there are strong relationships between economic growth and health and education systems. Through growth in economic, living standards and life expectancy for the developing nations certainly get better. With more fortunes poor nations are able to supply good health care services and sanitation to their people. In addition, the government of developing countries can provide more money for health and education to the poor, which led to decrease the rates of illiteracy. This is seen in many developing countries whose illiteracy rate fell recently. It is truth that, living standards and life expectancy of developing countries increase through economic gains from globalization. According to the World Bank (2004) " With globalization, more than 85 percent of the world's population can expect to live for at least sixty years and this is actually twice as long as the average life expectancy 100 years ago". In addition, globalization helped doctors and scientists to contribute to discover many diseases, which spread by human, animals and birds, and it helped them to created appropriate medicines to fight these deadly diseases. For example, HIV/ADIS, swine flu and birds' flu entire world know about these diseases and they know how to avoid it. By globalization, there are many international organizations, such as, Non-governmental Organization (NGO), World Health Organization (WHO) and UNESCO, trying to eliminate illiteracy and deadly diseases in the world and save the life. Despite these positive effects of globalization to the education and health fields in the developing countries. However, globalization could have negative impacts also in these fields; globalization facilitates the spread of new diseases in developing nations by travelers between countries. Due to increased trade and travel, many diseases like HIV/ADIS, Swine Flu, Bird Flu and many plant diseases, are facilitated across borders, from developed nations to the developing ones. This influences badly to the living standards and life expectancy these countries. According to the World Bank (2004) "The AIDS crisis has reduced life expectancy in some parts of Africa to less than 33 years and delay in addressing the problems caused by economic". Another drawback of globalization is, globalized competition has forced many minds skilled workers where highly educated and qualified professionals, such as scientists, doctors, engineers and IT specialists, migrate to developed countries to benefit from the higher wages and greater lifestyle prospects for themselves and their children. This leads to decrease skills labor in the developing countries.

3- Culture Effects

Globalization has many benefits and detriment to the culture in the developing countries. Many developing countries cultures has been changed through globalization, and became imitate other cultures such as, America and European countries. Before globalization it would not have been possible to know about other countries and their cultures. Due to important tools of globalization like television, radio, satellite and internet, it is possible today to know what is happening in any countries such as, America, Japan and Australia. Moreover, people worldwide can know each other better through globalization. For example, it is easy to see more and more Hollywood stars shows the cultures different from America. In addition, today we can see clearly a heavily effect that caused by globalization to the young people in the different poor nations, it is very common to see teenagers wearing Nike T-Shirts and Adidas footwear, playing Hip-Hop music, using Apple iPad and iPhone and eating at MacDonald, KFC and Domino's Pizza. It is look like you can only distinguish them by their language. One the other hand, many developing countries are concerned about the rise of globalization because it might lead to destroy their own culture, traditional, identity, customs and their language. Many Arab countries such as Iraq, Syria, Lebanon and Jordan, as developing countries have affected negatively in some areas, their cultures, Developing Country Studies www. iiste.org customs and traditional have been changed. They wear and behave like developed nations, a few people are wearing their traditional cloths they used to. Furthermore, globalization leads to disappearing of many words and expressions from local language because many people use English and French words. In addition, profound changes have taken place in the family life, young people trying to leave their families and live alone when they get 18 years old, and the extended family tends to become smaller than before (Kurdishglobe, 2010).

Conclusion

In conclusion, as we can see, the process of globalization has involved all the countries around the world. Developing countries such as India, China, Africa, Iraq, Syria, Lebanon and Jordan have been affected by globalization, and whether negatively or positively, the economies of these countries have improved under the influence of globalization. The size of direct foreign investment has increased and a lot of unhealthy habits and traditions erased, but also globalization has brought many drawbacks to these countries as well. Many customs and cultures are disappeared such as traditions clothes and some language and expressions have changed. In addition, the violence and drugs abuse are increased and a lot of deadly diseases have spread under the influence of globalization. However, although globalization has many disadvantages, we believe that globalization has brought the developing countries many more benefits than the detriments. For example, we can see there is more and a biggest opportunity for people in both developed countries and developing countries to sell as many goods to as many people as right now, so we can say this is the golden age for business, commerce and trade.

One of the major potential benefits of globalization is to provide opportunities for reducing macroeconomic volatility on output and consumption via diversification of risk. The overall evidence of the globalization effect on macroeconomic volatility of output indicates that although direct effects are ambiguous in theoretical models, financial integration helps in a nation's production base diversification, and leads to an increase in specialization of production. However, the specialization of production, based on the concept of comparative advantage, can also lead to higher volatility in specific industries within an economy and society of a nation. As time passes, successful companies, independent of size, will be the ones that are part of the global economy.

6.2 The View from the Penthouse

For business leaders and members of the economic elite, globalization is good. Cheaper labor overseas enables them to build production facilities in locations where labor and healthcare costs are low, and then sell the finished goods in locations where wages are high.

Profits soar due to the greatly reduced wages for workers, and Wall Street rewards the big profit gains with higher stock prices. The CEOs of global companies also get credit for the profits. Their rewards are usually generous compensation packages, in which company stock and stock options figure prominently. Institutional investors and wealthy individuals also take home the big gains when stock prices increase.

6.3 The View from the Street

But globalization doesn't only affect CEOs and high-net-worth individuals. Competition for jobs stretches far beyond the immediate area in a global marketplace. From technology call centers in India, to automobile manufacturing plants in China, globalization means that workers must compete with job applicants from around the world.

Some of these changes arose because of the North American Free Trade Agreement (NAFTA). NAFTA sent the jobs of U.S. autoworkers to Mexico, a developing country, where wages are significantly lower than those in the U.S. A few years later, some of those same jobs were relocated to third-world countries in East Asia, where wages are even lower.

In both cases, the auto manufacturers expected U.S. consumers to continue buying those products at U.S. prices. While critics of globalization decry the loss of jobs that globalization can entail for developed countries, those who support globalization argue that the employment and technology that is brought to developing countries helps those populations toward industrialization and the possibility of increased standards of living.

6.4 The View from the Middle Ground

In the globalization battleground, outsourcing is a double-edged sword. On the one hand, low wages in foreign countries enable retailers to sell clothing, cars and other goods at reduced rates in western nations where shopping has become an ingrained part of the culture. This allows companies to increase their profit margins. At the same time, shoppers save money when they buy these goods, causing some supporters of globalization to argue that while sending jobs overseas tends to lower wages, it may also lower prices at the same time.

Lower-income workers also enjoy some of the benefits of stock price appreciation. Many workers have mutual funds holdings, particularly in their 401(k) plans. When companies outsource jobs and get rewarded with rising share prices, mutual funds with those shares also increase in value.

6.5 The Effects of Globalization

The ever-increasing flow of cross-border traffic in terms of money, information, people and technology isn't going to stop. Some argue that it is a classic situation of the rich get richer while the poor get poorer. While global standards of living have risen overall as industrialization takes root in third-world countries, they have fallen in developed countries. Today, the gap between rich and poor countries is expanding, as is the gap between the rich and poor within these countries.

Homogenization of the world is another result, with the same coffee shop on every corner and the same big-box retailers in seemingly every city in every country. So, while globalization does promote contact and exchange between cultures, it also tends to make them more similar to one another. At the market level, linked global financial markets propel local issues into international problems, such as meltdowns in Southeast Asia and the 1998 Russian debt default.

6.6 What Lies Ahead?

Deviation from the status quo on this issue is likely to be minimal. The massive outsourcing of U.S. manufacturing jobs that began decades ago continues today. White collar jobs, such as call center workers, medical technicians and accountants have also joined the outsource parade, leaving many to argue that those profiting from the arrangement have little incentive to change it, while those most impacted by it are virtually powerless.

Politicians have latched onto the idea of the disappearing middle class as a political issue, but none of their income redistribution schemes are likely to have any immediate substantial impact.

6.7 The Bottom Line

Public scrutiny of CEO compensation has encouraged business leaders to begin to see that a rising tide doesn't necessarily lift all boats. In many cases, low-wage workers get hurt the most because they don't have transferable skills. The concept of retraining workers is on the radar, but it's easier said than done and decades too late for the American manufacturing industry. Until a better solution is found, education, flexibility and adaptability are the keys to survival. So far, the only answer that politicians and business leaders agree on is the value of an educated, flexible, adaptable workforce.

6.8 Legal

A common analogy is that "ethics begin where the law ends"; meaning that there are many things that are not illegal that should not be widespread practice. This is the essence of ethics.

The more economic transactions lose their connection to a region, the more they escape the control of the respective national governments. As soon as a company leaves it home territory and moves part of its operation to a third world country, the legal framework becomes vastly different. Laws on employee protection, health and safety, environmental impact tend to be laxer in developing economies and offer unethical businesses a framework to reduce costs through dropping standards.

A key point is that global financial markets are largely beyond the control of any national government (and their laws to an extent), so we need to consider the ethics of those who do exert control in these markets.

6.9 Accountability

Multinational Corporations (MNC's) own the mass media that influence much of the information and entertainment we are exposed to, they supply global products, they pay our salaries, and they pay much of the taxes that keep governments running. In 2008 Wal-Mart's revenue was about the same as the GDP of Greece (about $400Bn). Whereas the Greek government has to be accountable to the Greek people and must face elections on a regular basis, the executive of Wal-Mart is accountable only to a relatively small number of investors. Communities who rely on Wal-marts investment decisions (open / close stores, aggressive pricing to remove competitors) are disconnected and have no mechanism of influence on decision making.

To close; the more economic activity is reterritorialized, the less governments can control them, and the less they are open to democratic control of the affected people. Put simply, globalization leads to a growing demand for corporate accountability.

6.10 Decreased Employment

The influx of foreign companies into developing countries increases employment in many sectors, especially for skilled workers. However, improvements in technology come with the new businesses and that technology spreads to domestic companies. Automation in the manufacturing and agricultural sectors lessens the need for unskilled labor and unemployment rises in those sectors. If there is no infrastructure to help the unemployed train for the globalized economy, social services in the country may become strained trying to care for the new underclass.

7. REFERENCES

1. Bentley, Jerry H. 1993. *Old World Encounters: Cross-Cultural Contacts and Exchanges in Pre-Modern Times.* Oxford University Press. ISBN 0195076400.

2. Bhagwati, Jagdish. 2004. *In Defence of Globalization.* Oxford University Press. ISBN 0195170253.

3. Findlay, Ronald. 2002. "Globalization and the European Economy: Medieval Origins to the Industrial Revolution." In Henry Kierzkowski (ed.). *Europe and Globalization.* Palgrave Macmillan. ISBN 978-0333998397.

4. Friedman, Thomas. 2000. *The Lexus and the Olive Tree.* ISBN 0374185522.

5. Gilpin, Robert. 2001. *Global Political Economy: Understanding the International Economic Order.* Princeton University Press. ISBN 0691086761.

6. Hardt, Michael, and Antonio Negri. 2000. *Empire*. ISBN 0674006712.

7. Held, David, et. al. 1999. *Global Transformations: Politics, Economics, and Culture*. Stanford University Press. ISBN 0804736278.

8. Hirst, Paul Q., and Grahame Thompson. 1996. *Globalization in Question*. Polity Press. ISBN 0745621643.

9. King, Anthony. 1997. *Culture: Globalization and the World-System*. University of Minnesota Press. ISBN 0816629536.

10. Klein, Naomi. 2001. *No Logo*. ISBN 0006530400.

11. Legrain, Philippe. 2002. *Open World: The Truth About Globalization*. ISBN 034911644X.

12. Martin, Hans-Peter. 1996. *The Global Trap: Globalization and the Assault on Prosperity and Democracy (Die Globalisierungsfalle)*. ISBN 1856495302.

13. McLuhan, Marshall. 1960. *Explorations in Communication*. Edited by E.S. Carpenter. Beacon Press. ASIN B000HY3XSA

14. McLuhan, Marshall. 2011. *The Gutenberg Galaxy: The Making of Typographic*

Man. University of Toronto Press. ISBN 978-1442612693.

15. Ransom, David. 1975. *The Trojan Horse: A Radical Look at Foreign Aid*.

16. Robertson, Roland. 1992. *Globalization: Social Theory and Global Culture*. Sage Publications. ISBN 0803981822.

17. Roy, Arundhati. 2004. *An Ordinary Person's Guide To Empire*. South End Press. ISBN 0896087271.

18. Rupert, Mark. 2000. *Ideologies of Globalization: Contending Visions of a New World Order*. Routledge Publishers. ISBN 041518925.

19. Steger, Manfred. 2003. *Globalization: A Very Short Introduction*. Oxford University Press. ISBN 019280359X.

20. Stiglitz, Joseph. 2002. *Globalization and Its Discontents*. ISBN 014101038X.

21. Tomlinson, John. 1999. *Globalization and Culture*. University of Chicago Press. ISBN 0226807681.

22. Weatherford, Jack. 2004. *Genghis Khan and the Making of the Modern World*. Three Rivers Press. ISBN 0609809644.

23. Wolf, Martin. 2005. *Why Globalization Works.* ISBN 978-0300107777.

1.1. External links

All links retrieved April 2016.

1. Yale Global Online
2. Free Trade and Globalization — discusses the negative aspects of globalization, WTO and many others related to globalization
3. Priority Wire — A daily source of news on globalization, corporate power, sustainable development, and global poverty/disease.
4. Globalism/Anti-globalism - The main points of a debate
5. Stanford Encyclopedia of Philosophy entry on Globalization
6. Globalization: The Socialist Perspective
7. The Globalist | Front Page
8. http://www.ibtimes.co.uk/videos/promotion ?utm source=ibtimes&utm campaign =ibtus&utm medium=IBT&fq score =0&ref=http%253A%252F%252Fwww.ibtimes.

co.uk%252Fhow-president-trump-will-affect-global-economy-1590648

9. http://www.russia-direct.org/opinion/us-presidential-election-could-change-current-globalization-model

10. http://yaleglobal.yale.edu/content/us-election-world-special-report-yaleglobal

11. http://www.ibtimes.co.uk/how-president-trump-will-affect-global-economy-1590648

12. https://www.youtube.com/watch?v=JFisiNE5xUI

13. https://www.youtube.com/watch?v=TJtskViDg7g

14. https://www.youtube.com/watch?v=HNF7IVqidHo

15. https://www.youtube.com/watch?v=s8VOM8ET1WU

16. https://check-risk.com/global-economy-will-impact-the-2016-us-presidential-election/

17. https://www.ml.com/articles/how-presidential-elections-affect-the-markets.html

18. https://www.project-syndicate.org/commentary/us-presidential-candidates-economic-proposals-by-michael-boskin-2016-02?barrier=true

ABOUT THE AUTHOR AND HIS LIFE EXPERIENCE

This is my second book, and it embraces both sides of my lifelong interest and research, in practical terms endorses on the problems, opportunities threats and challenges which we face individually or collectively, and the theoretical side, seeking the contours of reality which exists in the development of business world Globally. My First Book "ORGANIZATIONAL RESTRUCTURING "has been very successful over the six continents.

Just a very brief summary of my professional career, left India in 1966, just after my Graduation and then completed all my further studies in UK and USA. I was awarded PHD from USA and never thought this experience would be the catalyst to my achievements for all my writing!

My professional career has spanned over few decades and has involved me living and working in a number of different countries. Worked in different multinational companies such as relates to international Banking for few years, After leaving the Bank I started an export and import business in textiles for which I spent a great deal of time in the Far East. During the same time, I ventured into the retail business in UK and had few stores before selling these to move on to other opportunities. I then moved into manufacturing clothing for the mass market of USA and UK. I set up a large manufacturing plant in the UAE to exploit the quota system that was in supported place in the 1990's. Things changed in 2001 when China returned to open free trade and as the UAE could no longer compete with the emerging markets, the business was trimmed down and moved back to UK and started Health care business, property business which have been running well over these years and during this time I entered into the Golf Business in many forms. Now I got addicted to this business and want to take this further in India, My ambition is to Bring Golf to the coming generation in India and bring Indian Golf to the world map.

Since my semi-reirement, I have pursued my passion for Golf in the interest of philanthropy, I founded the annual Yash International Charity Golf Day in aid of Cancer Research UK, and have been a very successful fund raiser for this charity ever since. This year we will be celebrating fourteen years since its inception.

During the last few years, while I was working on this book, I was fortunate to attend one meeting in Orlando on Globalization. Where many of the issues I was exploring were discussed by many of the intellectual people and authorities in various fields. I am grateful to the International Forum on Globalization for inviting me to participate in two of their intensive and highly informative teach-in on Globalization, while I was working on this book, I had the valuable opportunity to present ideas to the international audiences at this gathering.

In the course of my work on this book, I have had many opportunities to discuss new ideas about Globalization. Especially in the present climate conditions as these exist in the Global Village. In this book I propose to extend the new understanding of Globalization that has emerged from complexity theory to the social domain, To do so, I present a conceptual framework that integrates cultural ,cognitive and social dimensions. No time has not ceased and space has not vanished, but life does seem to be moving rapidly that way. Taken together, telecommunications, satellites, computers, and fibre optics are halving the cost of processing, storing, and transmitting information every eighteen minutes.

The global village even has its own market square in the shape of the Internet—a forum for commerce, information, entertainment, and personal interaction that makes previously undreamed of access to information available almost instantly and at extraordinarily low cost. Estimates suggest that 3.5 billion people around the world use the Internet already with the number rising every day 51% of the whole workload, Global Village is not only the Internet and telecommunications, it is also the more traditional fare of economists: trade in goods and trade in assets. The theoretical case for free trade is that it permits countries to concentrate on activities in which they enjoy comparative advantage and subjects firms to the healthy discipline of foreign competition. This means higher productivity and increased living standards, while consumers enjoy access to a wider variety of goods and services at lower cost. This is true not only in theory, it is true also in practice. Our post–World War II prosperity is based in large part on the rapid expansion of international trade in goods and services, which year after year has grown more rapidly than production. The theoretical argument for the free movement of capital is essentially the same as the argument for free trade in goods. Money can be channeled to its most profitable uses worldwide, financing productive investment opportunities even where domestic savings are scarce. However, the recent crises have made that a more controversial proposition.

Scholars argue that academic publications promote myths like 'globalization leads to one healthy world culture', 'globalization brings prosperity to person and planet', or 'global markets spread naturally'. They argue that globalization ideals represent primarily westernized perspectives. They further assert that management educators have given little thought to the fact that not everyone wants to be a member of a global village. These experts argue that it is important for scholars and citizens to balance unbridled enthusiasm for capitalism with evidence of its results. They call for an open and egalitarian dialogue among those who promote globalization, and those who believe it has negative consequences.

Current Global challenges demand concerted efforts by all conscious individual's in this Global Village, well informed and effective action that are optimized for maximum constructive impact. The whole Global Village is facing surmounting problems whether they are related to economy or climate change, terrorism etc. and lot other wide variety of problems. There are numerous barriers that impair their ability to act on their vision and motivation.

What this Global Village need is two throng approaches, one where all the world leaders join forces on urgent basis to come to the rescue or to aid of the most immediately endangered population of this Global Village and create a world level organization to monitor the threats, understand the economic needs of the people, understand their local Govt's role and look whole variety of issues, and create a Global Governance structure.

In this Global Village, we have seven and half Billion Humans on this planet, they all have different ways of interacting with each other, publicly, privately and Globally. Global human brains has a significant role to play in the fundamentals of transformation, of business, economy and different segments of the seven and half billion humans.

CPSIA information can be obtained
at www.ICGtesting.com
Printed in the USA
LVHW091912220323
742314LV00035B/1027